THE OLD FLUTE-PLAYER

A ROMANCE OF TO-DAY

EDWARD MARSHALL
AND CHARLES T. DAZEY

1st WORLD
LIBRARY
Literary Society

The Old Flute-Player

Edward Marshall and Charles T. Dazey

© 1st World Library, 2008
PO Box 2211
Fairfield, IA 52556
www.1stworldlibrary.com
First Edition

LCCN: 2007935372

Softcover ISBN: 978-1-4218-9325-9
Hardcover ISBN: 978-1-4218-9425-6
eBook ISBN: 978-1-4218-9225-2

Purchase *"The Old Flute-Player"*
as a traditional bound book at:
www.1stWorldLibrary.com/purchase.asp?ISBN=978-1-4218-9325-9

1st World Library is a literary, educational organization
dedicated to:

- Creating a free internet library of downloadable ebooks

- Hosting writing competitions and offering book publishing
scholarships.

Interested in more 1st World Library books? contact:
literacy@1stworldlibrary.com
Check us out at: www.1stworldlibrary.com

1st World Library Literary Society

Giving Back to the World

"If you want to work on the core problem, it's early school literacy."

- James Barksdale, former CEO of Netscape

"No skill is more crucial to the future of a child, or to a democratic and prosperous society, than literacy."

- Los Angeles Times

"Literacy... means far more than learning how to read and write... The aim is to transmit... knowledge and promote social participation."

- UNESCO

"Literacy is not a luxury, it is a right and a responsibility. If our world is to meet the challenges of the twenty-first century we must harness the energy and creativity of all our citizens."

- President Bill Clinton

"Parents should be encouraged to read to their children, and teachers should be equipped with all available techniques for teaching literacy, so the varying needs and capacities of individual kids can be taken into account."

- Hugh Mackay

CHAPTER I

Herr Kreutzer was a mystery to his companions in the little London orchestra in which he played, and he kept his daughter, Anna, in such severe seclusion that they little more than knew that she existed and was beautiful. Not far from Soho Square, they lived, in that sort of British lodgings in which room-rental carries with it the privilege of using one hole in the basement-kitchen range on which to cook food thrice a day. To the people of the lodging-house the two were nearly as complete a mystery as to the people of the orchestra.

"Hi sye," the landlady confided to the slavey, M'riar, "that Dutch toff in the hattic, 'e's somethink in disguise!"

"My hye," exclaimed the slavey, who adored Herr Kreutzer and intensely worshiped Anna. She jumped back dramatically. "*Not bombs!*"

The neighborhood was used to linking thoughts of bombs with thoughts of foreigners whose hair hung low upon their shoulders as, beyond a doubt, Herr Kreutzer's did, so M'riar's guess was not absurd. England offers refuge to the nightmares of all Europe's political indigestion. Soho offers most of them their lodgings. For years M'riar had been vainly waiting, with delicious fear, for that terrific moment when she should discover a loaded bit of gas-pipe in some bed as she yanked off the covers. Now real drama seemed, at last, to be coming into her dull life. Somethink in disguise—Miss Anna's father! She hoped it was *not* bombs, for bombs *might* mean trouble for him. She resolved that should she see a bobby trying to get up into the attic she would pour a kettleful of boiling water on him.

The landlady relieved her, somewhat, by her comment of next moment. "'E's too mild fer bombs by 'arf," she said, with rich disgust. "Likelier 'e's drove away, than that 'e's one as wishes 'e could drive. *Hi* sye, fer guess, that 'e's got titles, an' sech like, but's bean cashiered." (The landlady had had a son disgraced as officer of yeomanry and used a military term which, to her mind, meant exiled.) "'E's got that look abaht 'im of 'avin' bean fired hout."

"No fault o' 'is, then," said the slavey quickly, voicing her earnest partisanship without a moment's wait. She even looked at her employer with a belligerent eye.

"'E *doos* pye reg'lar," the landlady admitted with an air which showed that she had more than once had tenants who did not.

"Judgin' from 'is manners an' kind 'eart 'e *might* be *princes*," said the slavey, drawing in her breath exactly as she would if sucking a ripe orange.

"An' 'is darter might be princesses!" exclaimed the landlady with a sniff. Quite plainly she did not approve of the seclusion in which Herr Kreutzer kept his daughter. "Five years 'ave them two lived 'ere in this 'ere 'ouse, an' not five times 'as that there man let that there 'aughty miss stir hout halone!"

"'Ow 'eavingly!" sighed the maid, who never, in her life, had

Edward Marshall and Charles T. Dazey

been cared for, at all, by anyone.

"'Ow fiddlesticks!" the landlady replied. "You'd think she might be waxworks, liable to melt if sun-shone-on! Fer *me*, *Hi* says that them as is too fine for Soho houghtn't to be *livin'* 'ere. That's w'at *Hi* says—halthough 'e pyes as reg'lar as clockworks."

"Clockworks fawther with a waxworks darter!" cried the slavey, who had a taste for humor of a kind. "Th' one 'ud stop if t'other melted. *That's* sure."

"'E hidolizes 'er that much hit mykes me think o' Roman Catholics an' such," the landlady replied.

Then, for a time, she paused in thought, while the slavey lost herself in dreams that, possibly, she had been serving and been worshiping a real princess. As the height of the ambition of all such as she, in London, is to be humble before rank, the mere thought filled her with delight and multiplied into the homage of a subject for an over-lord the love she felt already for the charming German girl of whom they spoke.

"She *might* be," said the landlady, at length.

"W'at? Princesses?" inquired the wistful slavey.

The landlady looked shrewdly at her. It might be that by thus confiding to the servant her own speculations as to her lodgers' rank, she had been sowing seed of some extravagance. Hypnotized by the idea, the slavey might slip to the two mysterious Germans, sometime, something which would not be charged upon the bill! "Nothink of the sort!" she cried, therefore, hastily. "An' don't you never tyke no coals to 'em that you don't tell abaht—you 'ear?"

The slavey promised, but the seed was sown. From that time on full many a small attention fell to the Herr Kreutzer and his pretty, gentle-mannered, dark-haired, big-eyed Anna of which the landlady knew nothing, and many a dream of romance did the smutted slavey's small, sad eyes see in the kitchen fire on lonely evenings while she was waiting for the last lodger to come in before she went to bed behind the kindlings-bin. And the central figures of these dreams were, always, the beautiful young German girl and her dignified, independent, shabby, courteous old father.

In the small orchestra where Kreutzer played, he made no friends among the other musical performers; when the manager of the dingy little theatre politely tried to pump him as to details of his history he managed to evade all answers in the least illuminating, although he never failed to do so with complete politeness.

All that really was known of him was that he had arrived in London, years ago, with only two possessions which he seemed to value, and, indeed, but two which were worth valuing. One of these, of course, was his exquisite young daughter, then a little child; the other was his wonderful old flute. The daughter he secluded with the jealous care of a far-eastern parent; the flute he played upon with an artistic skill unequalled in the history of orchestras in that small theatre.

With it he could easily have found a place in the best orchestra in London, but, apparently, he did not care to offer such a band his services. On the one or two occasions when a "cruising listener" for the big orchestras came to the little theatre, heard the old man's masterful performance, found himself enthralled by it and made the marvelous flute-player a rich offer, the old man refused peremptorily even to talk the matter over with him—to the great delight of the small manager, who was paying but a pittance for his splendid work.

Edward Marshall and Charles T. Dazey

So anxious did Herr Kreutzer seem to be to keep from winning notice from the outside world, indeed, that when a stranger who might possibly be one of those explorers after merit in dim places appeared there in the little theatre, the other members of the orchestra felt quite sure of wretched playing from the grey-haired flutist. If it chanced that they had noticed no such stranger, but yet Herr Kreutzer struck false notes persistently, they all made sure that they had missed the entrance of the "cruiser," searched the audience for him with keen and speculative eyes and played their very best, certain that the man was there and hopeful of attracting the attention and the approbation which the old flute-player shunned. More than one had thus been warned, to their great good.

And Herr Kreutzer, on such evenings, was privileged to strike false notes with painful iteration, even to the actual distress of auditors, without a word of criticism from the leader or the manager. Excruciating discord from the flute, on three or four nights of a season, was accepted as part payment for such playing, upon every other night, as seldom had been heard from any flute in any orchestra in London or elsewhere.

The theatre saw very little of the daughter. Once at the beginning of the run of every fit new play, the flute-player requested of the manager a box and always got it. In this box, on such occasions, his daughter sat in solitary state, enjoying with a childish fervor the mumming of the actors on the stage, the story of the play, the music of the orchestra. Such glimpses, only, had the theatre of her. Her father never introduced her to an attache of the establishment. Once, after she had grown into magnificent young womanhood, he very angrily refused an earnest supplication for an introduction from the manager, himself. On the nights when she came to the theatre he took her to the box, before the overture began, and she sat there, quite alone, until he went to her after the audience had been "played out."

His own exclusiveness was very nearly as complete. He formed no intimacies among the members of the orchestra with whom he played eight times a week, although his face showed, sometimes, that he yearned to join their gossip, in the stuffy little room beneath the stage, which housed them when they were not in their places in the crowded space "in front" allotted to them.

"*Tiens!*" said the Frenchman who played second-violin. "Ze ol' man have such fear zat we should wiss to spik us wiz 'is daughtaire, zat 'e trit us lak we 'ave a seeckness catchable!"

It was almost true. He did avoid the chance of making her acquainted with any of the folk with whom his daily routine threw him into contact, with a care which might suggest a fear of some sort of contagion for her. But not all the members of the orchestra resented it. The drummer (who also played the triangle and tambourine when need was, imitated railway noises with shrewd implements, pumped an auto-horn when motor-cars were supposed to be approaching or departing "off-stage" and made himself, in general, a useful man on all occasions) was his firm friend and partisan.

"Garn, Frawgs!" he sneered, to the resentful Frenchman. "Yer 'yn't fit ter sye ther time o' dye ter 'er; yer knows yer 'yn't."

"Wat? To ze daughtaire of a flute!" the Second-Violin replied. "W'y—"

"Garn!" said the drummer. "Sye, yer myke me sick! You, with yer black-'aired fyce an' paytent boots! Hi bean 'ammerin' 'ide in horchestras since me tenth birthdye, but Hi knows a hangel w'en Hi sees one, an' lawst night Hi missed a 'ole bar on the snare fer lookin' up at 'er just once. Hi never see a brunette look so habsolutely hinnocent. Th' Ol' Nick's peekin' out o' brunettes' faces, somew'eres, mostly. Don't know w'at she myde me think of—m'ybe wreaths o' roses red an' pink, an' m'ybe crowns o' di'mun's—but Hi missed a 'ole bar on th' snare fer thinking somethink."

"*Tiens!*" the Frenchman began scornfully. "He is too much—"

"Garn!" said the drummer, threateningly, and it may be that the tinkle of the "ready" bell prevented something more than words between them, for the drummer, at the time, was holding the bass-drum-stick. He could have struck a mighty blow with it.

Just when the thought of leaving for America first began to grow in Kreutzer's mind, it would be hard to say, but it took definite form immediately subsequent to the London visit of a Most Exalted Personage from Prussia. On the last day of this Most Exalted Personage's stay Herr Kreutzer was enjoying, with his Anna, the long Sunday twilight in Hyde Park. They often strolled there of a Sunday evening. The Most Exalted Personage, being in a democratic mood and wishful of seeing London and its people quietly, was also strolling in Hyde Park and met the father and the daughter, face to face.

There was nothing, so far as Anna saw, about the stranger in plain *mufti*, to make her father drop his head, pull down his hat and hurry on, almost as if in sudden panic, dragging her by a slender wrist clasped in a hand which trembled; but he did do all these things, while the queer gentleman with the upturned moustaches (Anna had no notion who he was) stopped stonestill in his stroll and gazed after them with puzzled eyes in which a semi-recognition and a very lively curiosity seemed growing.

"Who is he, father?" Anna asked, in English, which the father much preferred to German from her lips and which she spoke with carefully exact construction, but with charming rolling of the r's and hissing of the s's. Her accent was much more pronounced than his, due, doubtless, to the fact that while he went daily to his little corner of the English world to earn their living, her seclusion was complete. She saw few English save M'riar and the landlady—whose accent never tempted her to imitation. "He seemed to know you," she went on. "He seemed to wish, almost, to speak with you, but seemed to feel not positive that you *were* you."

Kreutzer gave her a quick glance, then seemed to pull himself together with an effort. He assumed a carefully surprised air. "Who is he? Who is who, mine liebschen?"

"The gentleman from whom you ran away?"

"I run!" said Kreutzer, doubling his demeanor of astonishment as if in total ignorance of what she meant. "I run! Why should I run, my Anna? Why should I run from anybody?"

The daughter looked at him and sighed and then she looked at him and smiled, and said no more. So many times, in other days, had things like this occurred; so many times had she been quite unable to get any lucid exposition from him of the strange occurrences, that, lately, she never probed him for an explanation. She well knew, in advance, that she would get none, and was unwilling to compel him into laboring evasions. But such matters sorely puzzled her.

She did not learn, therefore, that the tall and handsome man who had so curiously stared at them was the Exalted Personage; she did not learn why it had been that from him

Kreutzer had fled swiftly with her, obviously worrying intensely lest they might be followed. She did not know why, later, she was in closer espionage than ever. Two or three days afterwards, when Kreutzer came in with his pockets full of steamship time-tables and emigration-agents' folders, she did not dream that it was that the Most Exalted Personage had cast his eyes upon them, rather than the fact that wonderful advantages were promised to the emigrant by all this steamship literature, which had made him make a wholly unexpected plan to go from London and to cross the mighty sea. He swore her to close secrecy.

It was with the utmost difficulty that she concealed their destination from the landlady and from the slavey who assisted her in packing the small trunks which held their all. She was always glad of anything which made it absolutely necessary for them to be with her, for her father, long ago, had told her not to ask them into their small rooms when their presence there was not imperatively needed. She was and had been, ever since she could remember clearly, very lonely, full of longing for companionship—so very full of longing that, had he not commanded it, she would not have been, as he was, particular about the social status of the friends she made.

Even poor M'riar's love was very sweet and dear to her, and now, as she was packing for departure the meagre garments of her wardrobe, her scanty little fineries, the few small keepsakes she had hoarded of the pitifully scarce bright days of her life (almost every one of these a gift from her old father, token of a birth-or feast-day) it was with a sudden burst of tears, a rushing, overwhelming feeling of anticipatory loneliness, that she looked at the grimy little child who was assisting her.

M'riar fell back on her haunches with a gasp. "Garn!" she

cried. "Garn, Miss! Don't yer dare to beller!"

A stranger might have thought she was impertinent, for "garn" on cockney lips means "go on, now," in the slang of the United States, and "beller" is not elegant, but Anna knew that she did not intend an impudence.

"I feel very sad at leaving you, M'ri-arrr." There was pathos, now, in the way Miss Anna rolled her r's.

"Sad! Huh! Hi thinks Hi'll die of it!" was the reply, accompanied by more choked sobs and many snuffles. "An' yer won't heven tell me w'ere yer hoff to!"

"I don't know, exactly, where we're off to M'ri-arrr. Some-where very far—oh, very far!"

M'riar, in spite of a firm resolution not to yield to tears, cast herself upon the floor in anguish, and, as she kicked and howled, grasped one of Anna's hands and kissed it, mum-bling it, as an anguished mother might a babe's—the hand of an exceedingly loved babe whom she expected, soon, to lose by having given it to someone in adoption.

At that time M'riar looked upon the separation as inevitable. The wild scheme which, afterwards, grew in her alert and worried brain, had not yet had its birth and she could not take the thought of her Miss Anna's going with composure.

"Hi didn't want ter 'oller," she said, at length, when she had regained her self-control, "but that there yell hinside o' me was bigger'n Hi 'ad room fer, Miss."

"It is very sweet of you to weep," said Anna gravely, "although it is not sweet to *hear* you weep; but I think it means you love me, M'ri-arrr, doesn't it?"

"Hi fair wusships yer," said M'riar. "Fair wusships yer."

And there was a strange thing about Miss Anna. It did not in the least surprise her to be told with an undoubted earnestness, indeed to know, that she was literally worshiped as a goddess might be. There was something in her blood which made this seem quite right and proper. She looked at the poor slavey with the kind eyes of a princess gazing at a weeping subject, whose suffering has come through loyalty, and kindly smiled.

"It is very nice of you, M'riarr. I am fond of you, M'riarr."

"I knows yer is; I knows yer is," said M'riar. "Tyke me with yer, won't yer, Miss?"

"Oh, I couldn't take you with me," Anna answered, as she laid a kind, if queenly hand upon the poor thing's cheek. "But you must let me know just where you are at all times, and, perhaps, some day, I will send you something to remind you of me."

"Hi won't need nothink ter remind me, Miss," said M'riar. "Hi'll remember yer, hall right."

The next morning came a four-wheeled cab up to the dingy door, to the vast amazement of the other lodgers, and, indeed, the entire neighborhood. Into this Herr Kreutzer handed his delightful daughter with as much consideration as a minister could show a queen, and then, with courtly bows, climbed in himself, having, with much ceremony, bade the landlady adieu. Anna cast a keen glance all about, expecting a last glimpse of M'riar, but had none and was grieved. So soon do the affections of the lower classes fade!

After the cab started, the Herr Kreutzer carefully pulled

down the blinds a little way, on both side windows, so that the inside of the cab was dark enough to make it impossible for wayfarers to note who was within.

"Father," said Anna, curiously, "why do you pull down the blinds?"

"Er—er—mine eyes. The light is—"

He did not complete the sentence.

"Father," she asked presently, "why did you change the tickets?"

"Change the tickets, Anna? I have not changed the tickets."

"But you told the landlady we were to sail from Southampton. The tickets, which you showed to me, say Liverpool."

"A little strategy, mine Anna; just a little strategy."

"I do not understand."

"No, liebschen; you do not," he granted gravely.

A moment later and the cab jounced over a loose paving-block, almost unseating M'riar from her place on the rear springs. The little scream she gave attracted the attention of the vehicle's two passengers and they peered from the window at the rear; but it was small and high and they did not catch sight through it of the strange, ragged little figure, with the set, determined face, which was clinging to their chariot with a desperate tenacity.

M'riar's feelings would have been difficult of real analysis and she did not try to analyze them, any more than a devoted dog who desperately follows his loved master when that master is not cognizant of it and does not wish it, tries to analyze the dog-emotions which compel him to cling to the trail. Such a dog knows quite enough, at such a time, to keep clear of his master's view, although his following is an expression of his love and though that love is born, he knows, of like love in his master's heart for him. M'riar was yielding to an uncontrolled, an uncontrollable impulse of love, and, though her brain was active with the cunning of the slums, had not the least idea of combatting it, or letting anything less strong than actual death would be in its deterrent force, prevent her from obeying the swift impulse to the very end. She had not taken any of her mistress' money, when she fled. Her only sin, she told herself, was leaving without notice. She had only made a little bundle of her own worn, scanty, extra clothes, which, now, was tied about her waist and hung beneath the skirt she wore. There were not many of those clothes, so the dangling bundle did not discommode her when she dodged behind the cab, ran beside it (on the far side from the lodging-house) till it turned a corner, and then sought her perch upon its springs behind. In her mouth were seven golden sovereigns, the hoard of her whole lifetime, barring some small silver and an Irish one-pound note stowed in her left stocking. Her right stocking had been darned till it was nowise to be trusted with one-eighth of her whole wealth. She had no dimmest thought of whither she was bound; she only knew that she would go, if Fate permitted, wherever Anna went, to serve her.

Arrived at the confusion of the railway station known as Waterloo, Herr Kreutzer helped his Anna from the cab, paid the cabman from his slender store of silver, hired a porter with another shilling to take all their luggage to the train and went to get their third-class railway tickets, keeping, meanwhile, a keen eye for anyone who looked to be a German of position, and noting with delight that in the crowd not one pair of moustaches stuck straight up beside its owner's nose. Slinking after him, at a slight distance, but near enough to hear quite all he said, came M'riar, and, when he had passed on, bought for herself a third-class ticket to Southampton. Her keen eyes fixed upon the backs of the two folk with whom, without their knowledge, she had cast her fortunes, she then went into the train-shed and found a place, at length, in the next carriage to the one which they had entered. Then she trained a wary eye out of the window, to make sure they did not change their minds and slip out and away without her knowledge before the train departed.

On the arrival in Southampton she waited in the railway carriage till she saw them started down the platform; then, again, she trailed them. Two minutes after the Herr Kreutzer had purchased steerage tickets on the *Rochester* for far America, M'riar had bought one for herself. When the German and his daughter reached the shore-end of the slightly-angled gang-plank leading to the steamer's steerage-deck (close it was beside the steeper one which led up to the higher and more costly portions of the ship) she was not far behind them, trailing, watchful, terrified by the ship's mighty warning whistle which reverberated in the dock-shed till her teeth were set a-chatter in an agony of fear of the mere noise.

At this point she nearly lost her self-control and let her quarries see her, for Herr Kreutzer, in his hurry and excite-ment, dropped one of his small hand-bags. Almost she sprang to pick it up for him, through mere working of her strong instinct to serve him. Indeed, she would have done so had it not been for a tall and handsome youth.

This young man's eyes, M'riar had been noting, had been closely fixed upon the lovely face of Anna, doubly lovely, flushed as it now was by the excitement of the start of a great journey. He sprang forward, picked up the handbag and presented it to the old German with a frank good-fellowship of courtesy which took not the least account of the mere fact that he, himself, was on the point of stepping to the gang-plank leading to the first-cabin quarters, while Kreutzer, obviously, was about to seek the steerage-deck. M'riar, with her sharp, small eyes, noted that the youth, strong, graceful, tall, sun-burned and distinctly wholesome of appearance, did not look at Kreutzer, as he did the little service, but at Anna.

"Reg'lar toff!" she muttered, gazing at him with frank admiration, quite impersonal.

An instant later she saw that when he turned back from the rough, unpainted gang-plank to the steerage-deck to the more exclusive bridge, railed, hung with canvas at the sides and carpeted with red, which led to the first-cabin quarters, a lady seized his arm with a proprietary grasp and spoke a little crossly to him because he had delayed to do this tiny service for the pair of steerage passengers.

"Rg'lar cat!" said M'riar, estimating her as quickly as she had appraised the youth. "She's 'is mother, but she's catty. Dogs 'ud 'ate 'er, Hi'll go bail."

Her attention was absorbed, then, by the great problem of getting by the officer who examined steerage-tickets, without being seen by Kreutzer and his daughter.

"W'ere's yer luggage?" asked the officer.

"Luggage! Huh!" said M'riar. "W'at would *Hi* want o' *luggage*? Think Hi'm a hactress startin' hout hon tour?"

"Tykes six poun' ten to land on t'other side," the officer went on, suspiciously. "'Yn't got that, nyther, 'ave yer?"

"Betcher bloomink heye Hi gawt it," said M'riar confidently, and stooped as if she would pull out her wealth to show him, then and there.

"Hin yer stawckin', eh?" the man said grinning.

That which had been in her mouth was spent for ticket, mostly, but a little still was in her hand. "W'ere'd yer think Hi'd 'ave it?" she asked scornfully. "Hin me roight hear?" Then she showed him what was in her fist.

"Garn aboard," the man said, grinning.

"'Yn't I?" she asked briskly, and, seeing that Herr Kreutzer and his Anna had passed quite out of sight into the ship's mysterious interior, went up the gang-plank hurriedly, fearing to lose sight of them. She did not realize that on an impulse she was starting to go a quarter of the way around the earth. She only knew that love, love irresistible, supreme, was drawing her to follow where they led. But notwith-standing that it was pure love which drew her, she told herself, as she went up the plank: "Hif they ketches me they'll 'eave me hoverboard an' give me to th' fish, like's not."

Twenty minutes later the great ship was swinging out into the harbor. In a dark passage on the steerage-deck cowered M'riar, for the first time in her life afloat, and wondering why the motion of the vessel seemed to make her wish to die; her white face, strained, frightened eyes and trembling hands marking her, to the experienced, unsympathetic eyes of the stern steerage-stewardess, an early victim of seasickness.

"Hi, w'ere's yer ticket?" that fierce female cried, and M'riar showed it to her, weakly, scarcely caring whether it entitled her to passage or condemned her to expulsion from the ship by a sharp toss overside.

"Garn in there," said the stewardess, studying the ticket and its bearer's symptoms simultaneously. "S'y, yer goin' ter be a nice sweet passenger to 'ave hon board, now 'yn't yer?"

"Hi'm goin' ter die," said M'riar with firm conviction and not at all appalled but rather pleased at thought of it.

"No such luck fer hus!" the stewardess replied. "Get *in* there, cawn't yer, before hit comes quite hon?"

So M'riar, long before the ship began to definitely feel even the gentle Channel sea, was thrust into retirement, willy, nilly, and immediately sought a bunk, absolutely without interest in anything, even in her own sad fate. All she wished to do was die, at once, and she had too little energy even to wish that very vividly. Miss Anna, Herr Kreutzer and the fine young man who had been kind to them, who, ten minutes earlier, had all been real and potent interests, dimmed into hazy phantoms of a bygone activity of mind.

"Oh,—ar-r-r-r-r-r!" M'riar groaned. "Th' bloomink ship is standin' on 'er bloody 'ead, yn't 'er?"

"Garn! Keep yer 'ead *flat*. Lay *down*," the stewardess replied, "er *you'll* be."

M'riar kept her head flat.

Out on the open deck, forward of the bridge, where, as well as aft, the vessel, like many of a bygone type was cut away, leaving the forward and after railings of the promenade-deck, like the barriers of a balcony, for the first-cabin passengers to peer across at their less lucky fellows of the steerage, Herr Kreutzer and his Anna, both bewildered, stood by their little pile of baggage, waiting for direction and assistance in searching out their quarters. Surrounding them a motley group of many nationalities was gathered. There were Germans, Swedes, some French, some Swiss, a group of heavy-browed and jowled Hungarians, a few anaemic, underfed young cockneys, and, dominating all, to the casual eye, because of their bright colors, a small group of Italians. To these the largest one among them was making himself clear.

"I," he was saying, "am Pietro Moresco. I have-a da nice political posish, an' nice-a barber-shop on Mulberry-a Strit. Some-a day I getta on da force—da pollis-force. Sure t'ing. I been-a home to see ma moth. I go-a back to make-a da more mon." He pulled out from his corded bundle of red quilts and coats and rugs some bottles of cheap wine. "I getta place for all you men." He was beginning, thus early in the voyage of these would-be citizens, to prepare to use them in the politics of his over-crowded ward in New York City. "Come-a! We drink-a to Americ. We drink-a to New York. New York da mos' reech-a place."

Catching sight of the bewildered beauty of poor Anna, and the no less bewildered dignity of Herr Kreutzer, being dazzled by the former, as was everyone in sight, and being quite as anxious to make friends among prospective German citizens as among those of his own country (a German vote is likely to be useful, now and then, on Mulberry Street) he offered her a cup, and, as she took it automatically, would have poured some wine into it with a gallant smile. Kreutzer took the cup out of her hand and passed it back to him.

"Bitte," he said, calmly. "I thank you. My daughter does not care for wine."

Moresco, angered, gave him a black scowl and took the cup.

"By Jove," said the youth who had, upon the dock, picked up

Herr Kreutzer's bag. He was standing on the promenade-deck, above, beside his very, very stately mother, who, over-dressed and full of scorn for the whole world, was complaining because her doctor's orders had suggested traveling upon so slow and old a ship. "There's that stunning little German girl down there. Isn't she a picture? Gee! Her old man wouldn't let her drink with that black dago—not that she wanted to. But bully for Professor Pretzel!" "How very vulgar!" said his mother, looking down at the small, animated scene before her with disfavor. "Mere immigrants."

"I s'pose *our* folks were, sometime," John Vanderlyn replied. "But isn't she a corker, mother?"

"John, your language is too shocking! Please see about our deck-chairs," Mrs. Vanderlyn replied.

CHAPTER II

Under a brilliant summer sky the ocean heaved in mighty swells. Anna, on one of the most delightful mornings of this ideal voyage to America, found the port side of the ship unpleasant, because of the sun's brilliance. From every tiny facet of the water, which a brisk breeze crinkled, the light flashed at her eyes with the quick vividness of electric sparks, and almost blinded her. Not even her graceful, slender, and (surprising on that steerage-deck) beautifully white hand, now curved against her brow, could so shade her vision as to enable her to look upon the sea in search of the far sail which the lookout in the crow's nest had just reported to the bridge in a long, droning hail. Her curiosity in the passing stranger had been aroused by the keen interest which the more fortunately situated, on the promenade-deck, above, had shown by crowding to their rail. They were, as she could see from her humbler portion of the ship, talking of the far craft interestedly; but from her station, owing either to its lack of altitude or to the more dazzling glitter of the sea, due to the differing angle of her vision, she failed to catch a glimpse of it. The glare made her give up the search.

She shrugged her small, plaid shawl about her shoulders to meet the wind's now freshening assaults, pulled her knitted hood a little closer all about her face to hide it, through some sort of instinct (the first-cabin folk, above, all through the voyage, had been wont to gaze down on the steerage passengers as if they were a sort of interesting animals), and made her way across the slowly heaving planks to starboard. Glancing quickly upward as she went, she colored gloriously, for looking down straight at her from behind the rail which edged the elevated platform of the prosperous, stood the youth who had picked up her father's bag as they had come on board, and whose eyes, since the first day of the voyage, she had found it wise to dodge if she would keep the crimson from her cheeks.

Not that there had been anything, at any time, in the youth's gaze which could offend; rather had there been in it that which bewitched and thrilled. There was not another girl upon that steerage-deck who would not have been immensely pleased by and who would not have shyly answered his admiring glances, had they turned toward her, although there probably was not a girl there who was other than quite sweet and pure. Purity and sweetness are no bars to answering a glance and giggling. But he paid no heed, at all, to pretty emigrants who would have been delighted by flirtatious glances. It may, in fact, have been because of the shy fright, not in the least resentful, but sweetly, girlishly embarrassed, with which Anna greeted his, whenever her eyes caught them, that he turned them toward her so exclusively and frequently. Admiring youth called to admiring youth in surreptitious glances from the high deck to the lower, and, it may be, from the steerage-deck up to the promenade.

But, although she found no slightest thing offensive in the young man's veiled, approving surveillance, Anna felt almost as if she were in flight from peril—some brand-new, delightful peril—as, now, she hurried out of range of it and sought her father where, by the after-hatch, he perched upon a great coiled cable staring, staring, staring out across the sea toward Germany, the land to which, a few days since, although his actual departure had been from English shores, his heart had said a passionate farewell.

If Anna, with her graceful form, her delicately-colored, healthful cheeks, her cleancut and dainty features, offered a strong contrast to the buxom German maidens, dark, big-eyed Italian girls and others of the many-nationed women-travelers upon that steerage-deck, her father offered as strong contrast to the men. Among the swart Italians, blonde, stupid-looking Swedes, Danes and Norwegians and fat, red-faced Germans of the male steerage company, his finely-chiselled features, pale and ascetic-looking in their frame of whitened hair, stood out with accentuated testimony to high breeding, right living and exalted aims. And there was another difference, but less pleasing. By this, the ninth day out from port, grief, born of leaving friends and childhood scenes had vanished from the faces of the other voyagers, and, under the influence of a moderately smooth sea and splendid, sparkling weather, their thoughts were busy with the new shores to which the voyagers were journeying, with expectations of great days. But on his face no glow of pleasant anticipation ever shone. The old man's eyes were always turned toward that dear Germany which, first, he had been forced to leave for London, and now was, by the stern necessities of life, obliged to go still further from. Rarely, since the voyage had begun, had he, when on deck, raised his gaze from the great vessel's churning wake, which stretched, he liked to think, straight back toward Germany, save when his daughter spoke to him and roused him, for a moment, from his black depression. It was as if that thread of foam was the one thing, brief, evanescent, futile, though it was, which bound him, now, to the only land he cared for. His face was that of one who passes into final exile. Only when his eyes were on his daughter's did the expression of suppressed grief and despondency go from them for a moment; but when they looked at her they lighted brilliantly with love.

He had found adjustment to his crude surroundings with the utmost difficulty. Poor he had been in London, but his work had been among musicians, and even cheap musicians have in them something better, finer, higher than the majority of human cattle in the steerage of this ship could show. He felt uncomfortably misplaced.

This had been apparent from the start to his most interested observer—the handsome youth of the first cabin, whose glances sometimes made the daughter's eyes dodge and evade. It added to that young man's growing conviction that the aged man and beautiful young girl were not at all of the same class as their enforced associates upon the steerage-deck.

He remarked upon this to the second officer of the ship, who was highly flattered by his notice and anxious to give ear. He, too, had given some attention to the old man and his daughter and agreed with Vanderlyn about their great superiority to their surroundings.

He would have agreed with Vanderlyn in almost anything, that second officer, for every year he met and talked with some few thousand passengers who said it was the longer voyage which had tempted them to the old *Rochester*, while rarely was he in the least convinced by what they said. With the Vanderlyns, who did not say it, he thought that it was truth. Money they obviously had in plenty, and, inasmuch as they were, therefore, such pronounced excep-tions to the rule, he spent what time with them he could. They were prosperous and yet they sailed by that slow ship, therefore they loved the sea. Of this he was convinced—and in his firm conviction was entirely wrong.

The real truth was that Mrs. Vanderlyn, made bold by the possession of her money, had thought it was the magic key which certainly would open every door for her. There were doors in New York City, which, coming from the West, she had been palpitantly anxious to pass through, and, to her amazement, she found that money would not open them. Then there had occurred to her the brilliant plan of conquering, first, the aristocracy of Europe, who, the newspapers had told her, bowed in great humility before the eagle on the Yankee gold-piece. To the doors with crests upon their paneling, abroad, she had therefore borne her golden key that summer, only to discover that it fitted their locks quite as ill as those upon Fifth Avenue. Her heart was saddened with the woe of failure. The second officer could not guess that, sore from buffetings from those who would have none of her, she had been glad to secure passage on this ten-day boat, where, during the long voyage, she could haughtily refuse to notice those of whom she would have none. She had searched for a place and found one where she could scorn as she had recently been scorned. Her soul was black-and-blue from snubs. She wished to snub. A climber, who had failed to climb the highest social ladder, the handsome, haughty lady found a certain satisfaction in sitting for ten days upon the very apex of another ladder—briefer, less important, very little, to be sure, but still a social ladder —and giving it a quick, sharp shake as humble people put their feet upon it timidly, bowing and smiling tentatively at her unresponsive person. It was a sort of balm to her sore soul so see them tumble metaphorically, upon their backs. Her demeanor on the *Rochester* was the demeanor of a princess among aliens whom she utterly despises. The Cook's tourists, traveling school-teachers and young married couples homeward-bound after modest European honeymoons, were plainly scum to her, and it gave her ardent joy to see that most of them were hurt when she impressed this on them mercilessly. It was safer for her son to talk about the interesting German couple to the second officer than it was for him to talk about them to his mother, but, lo! youth knows not wisdom.

"Mother," he suggested upon the sixth day out, "I want to have you come and see a fascinating couple on the steerage-deck."

"Another bride and groom?" she asked, in a bored voice. Brides and grooms had come to be monotonous. She had seen all sorts since she had started on this journey and now loathed the thought of newly married fellow-creatures. She could not understand why John's interest had been maintained in them.

He laughed. "No, not a bride and groom. The man is an old German, handsome and refined, evidently out of place upon the steerage-deck, the girl—she—why, mother, she's a peach. *She'd* be out of place 'most anywhere but on a throne!"

"How very vulgar, John," his mother answered with that cold assumption of superiority which had come to her with money. "I cannot see how even you can link the steerage-deck with thrones. Princesses do not travel steerage except between the covers of cheap books."

He laughed again. John Vanderlyn was clean and healthy-souled. He did not always take his mother (whom he idolized) too seriously.

"I didn't say she was a princess," he replied, "but she might well be. It was, however, rather the old man than the girl, though she is very beautiful and quite as much misplaced upon the steerage-deck as he is, that I wished to have you see." He was, it will be noted, learning something of diplomacy. "He has a magnificent old face—the face of a fine nature which has suffered terribly. I have seen him as he stood at the ship's rail, astern, watching the white wake as if every bubble on it was a marker on a tragic path. It is as if all he loved on earth except the girl—you ought to see him look at her!—lies at the far end of that frothy, watery trail."

"You become almost poetic!" she said without enthusiasm.

But, a day afterwards, she went with him and looked down at the steerage passengers, singling out the pair he meant without the slightest difficulty.

"What a distinguished-looking man he is!" said she, involuntarily.

"Isn't he?" said her delighted son.

The daughter was not on the deck, just then, and young Vanderlyn was politic enough to say nothing of her, merely talking of the old man's impressive bearing, asking his mother to help him speculate about his history.

"I don't wonder he attracted you," she granted. "He looks very interesting. I am sure he *has* a history."

Her gaze was so intent, that, in a few moments, it attracted the attention of Herr Kreutzer, and the youth, observing that he seemed annoyed and shamed, hurried her away. Instinctively he had felt the old man flinch; instinctively he knew his pride, already, had been sorely hurt by the necessity of "traveling steerage"; that as they gazed at him the handsome, white-haired, emigrant had felt that his dire poverty had made of him a curiosity.

The young man led his mother back to her rug-padded deck-chair, pleased by the result of the first step in what he had resolved must be a strategy of worth. In some way he must fix things so that properly and pleasantly he could get acquainted with that girl. This, he thought (not being a born prophet), could only be accomplished through his mother, and already he had plans for it indefinitely sketched out in his mind. Events were fated to assist him and do better for him than his mother could have done for him, but, of course, he did not know that then.

From the moment when he saw the dignified old German shrink before his mother's gaze the youth was careful to avoid appearances of curiosity. If either old man or young girl came into view while he stood at the rail, above the steerage-deck, he went away, though other passengers, attracted by the beauty of the girl, and the distinguished look of the old man, were less considerate and stared, to their distress. When, later, the young man saw his mother staring as the others did and as he had, himself, at first, he hesitantly spoke to her about it.

"Nonsense," she replied. "You give them credit for too much fine feeling. Attention doubtless flatters them. It always does such people."

That she had lost her first idea that the pair might be entitled to unusual consideration bothered him; but he feared, because of his great plan, to make too vehement defense, so only said, with studied mildness:

"They are not 'such people', I am sure. You yourself, at first, said they looked 'different.' It's hard luck, I'll bet a hat, and not a lack of brains, decency or real distinction that's forced them to herd down there with those cattle. I'll guarantee they know the whole thing about the little social game in Germany." He watched his mother closely, to see if the shot told, and was delighted when he saw it did.

"Yes; he really looks superior," she admitted. "I have no doubt their German is quite *perfect*. I wonder—perhaps he might, at one time, have been someone of distinct importance."

"I have no doubt of it. Anyone can see it makes him sore as a mashed thumb to have his poverty make him into a free side-show to be stared at on this old canal-boat. I've seen the 'Cookies' rubbering and making comments that I know he heard. He flushed red as beets and took his daughter somewhere where their gimlet stare could not bore to her. Those glass-eyed school-ma'ams actually drove them out of the fresh air!"

"He seems to make no friends among the steerage passengers, as all the others do."

"Those swine? They drive him crazy. The girl is constantly annoyed by men that try to sidle up to her. I've been half expecting the old man would bat that big Italian who's always talking New York politics—shoot him with whatever he has always with him in that queer, oval case, and throw him to the fish."

"I think that is some instrument—some music thing."

"Might be a flute."

"Perhaps he is some really great musician," Mrs. Vanderlyn said, speculatively. "They go everywhere in Germany. No doors are closed to them. It wouldn't be at all surprising for a musician to travel as he's doing. Such people are eccentric, and often so foolishly improvident. Something about music makes them so. But they worship them in Germany. They know the very *highest* people."

Her son grasped at the suggestion. "Funny, isn't it—how crazy all the lieber-deutchers are when they hear music! Hoch der Kaiser sets the pace, himself."

"Yes, I know he does," said Mrs. Vanderlyn, a little shocked by his irreverent way of making reference to Heaven's Chosen. "Poor things!" Her sympathy was quite aroused, now. She became quite certain that the steerage couple had highly influential friends abroad. "Would it please him, do you think, if I should show the daughter some attention?"

John knew that "some attention" from his mother to the emigrants would mean a course of open patronage and he didn't wish to have her try that on with that particular pair. He shook his head. "I don't believe they'd stand for it," he said. "But if you could do them some real kindness—a courtesy that wasn't—er—er—patronizing, it—"

He gazed thoughtfully at Mrs. Vanderlyn for a short moment and then thought better, even, of encouraging her thus much. He loved his mother dearly but felt certain that she would be sure to wound the strangers if she did anything whatever for them.

"Perhaps the best thing, after all," he said, "will be to let them, undisturbed, preserve the incognito which they evidently wish to keep in their misfortune." He had roused his mother's interest more keenly than he had thought was possible. He would do no more to rouse it. He could only hope that it might bear for him the fruit he wished—a pleasant way of gaining an acquaintance with the lovely girl. He knew that it was possible it might do otherwise and make a pleasant meeting harder, even, than it seemed to be at present, but he had had to take the chance. At any rate he had sufficiently excused himself, in her eyes, for any reasonable thing he might, himself, do, when the opportunity occurred, to gain the friendship of the steerage travelers.

As for himself, he now carefully avoided any appearance of observing them. In one way or another he watched them a good deal, but he did so with such care that he was certain they were unaware of it—at least was certain that the old man did not notice it. He found his heart athrob with quite unusual speed, when, once or twice, he saw the girl's big eyes directed toward him, not resentfully. They were, he thought, the most resplendent eyes which ever had been turned in his direction, but he did not let her know that he observed her glances.

His interest continually deepened, and the voyage, which he had thought would be a tiresome trip, became one of the most absorbing journeys he had ever known. Memories of those eyes were with him, even when he was beyond the shy range of their timid glances. When, at the ship's bow, he gazed over at the sporting dolphins or watched the water curving gracefully from the black prow, they floated in the sea, alluringly. If he turned his glance above to watch the fleecy clouds which were the only vapors in the sky upon this ideal crossing, they shaped themselves into her profile, the azure of the sky lost by comparison with that which glowed serene from her great eyes. John Vanderlyn was really dismayed to find that they were everywhere. He had not been susceptible, as youths go, in the past; now he found himself enthralled, spellbound by the appeal of this small German girl who traveled cheaply in the steerage of a slow ship toward America, a part of a large company of needy aliens seeking a new home in what they thought the land of promise.

As the voyage neared its end he saw with some dismay that

the old man had managed to make enemies among the emigrants by his aloofness. The sea was very smooth, these days, and, under smiling skies the steerage-deck was swarming. The stewardess announced that but one of all the seasick passengers, a young English girl, was left in the infirmary; the only other call for the ship's doctor came from a mother for her tiny babe of two or three months which had been stricken with some increasing ailment before they had embarked upon the ship. The emigrants were making merry daily, from early morning until nine or ten of evenings; there were few moments when from their part of the ship some crude music was not rising.

Concertinas, mouth-organs, a badly-mastered violin gave forth their notes from time to time, their harshness softened by the mingling of the waves' lap on the vessel's sides. Now and then the first-class passengers looked down with amused curiosity upon rude dances, the dancers' merriment enhanced by stumbling lurches born of the vessel's slow, long rollings on the sea's vast, smooth-surfaced swells.

The old man and his daughter never joined in these crude pleasurings and John found in this a certain comfort which he did not try to analyze. His mother, also watching now and then, observed it, too, and felt her interest in them increasing. Two days before the slow old ship was due to reach New York she had almost made her mind up to investigate the pair. Should she find that they were worthy, she told John (that is, should she find they could, in any way, be useful in her campaign of next summer, which, already, she was planning) she might try to help them in New York. Her resentment of John's interest in them had faded. If they were ordinary emigrants he would not see them after the ship docked, if they were of enough importance to be useful to her, if they had influential friends abroad, the more he saw of them the better. Mrs. Vanderlyn was not a mercenary woman. The only gold she worshiped had been beaten into coronets; of that which had been minted she had plenty. She did not envy fortunes, though her envy of position was unbounded.

"You might make a little inquiry," she told her son. "If they should really have friends among the aristocracy—"

It both amused and angered him. He had imbibed, at a small western college and in the little taste of business life which he had had in New York City, a wondrous spirit of democracy which his stay in Europe had by no means lessened. It was not the man's potential social usefulness which made appeal to him, it was the soul which he saw shining, clear and lovely, in his daughter's eyes; it was not the father's slow, grey dignity which made him wish to help him, it was the long, pathetic gaze, which, from time to time, he saw him cast back along the vessel's wake, the lines of patiently-borne sorrow which had formed about his fine, strong mouth, the stoop of weariness and woe endured with uncomplaining fortitude which bent his shoulders. He might be of an artistic worth which made him peer of and received by kings—of that John Vanderlyn knew nothing and cared less; but that he was a gentleman of lofty mind and many sorrows patiently endured he felt quite certain, and, as such, his heart yearned to him. He would have been delighted if some way had come to help him, but he could not bring himself to such a curious investigation of his poor affairs as his mother would have had him make with prying inquiries. It seemed to him that such a course would be impertinent, and so, whenever she suggested it, he temporized and hesitated.

As the voyage progressed, too, it was plain enough that others than the Vanderlyns began to feel, instinctively, the real superiority of the old man and his daughter. Down on the steerage-deck they were, involuntarily, given a certain courteous consideration by the passengers, and even by the stewards—and to impress a steerage-steward is no ordinary victory. The old man showed a kindly heart, especially to the many women with small babes among the huddled passengers. Love of children, plainly, was mighty in his soul and by the hour he sat, surrounded by a circle of the little ones, to their very great delight and the relief of the poor mothers who thus obtained the first hours of freedom from continual care which they had had since the long voyage had begun.

It was his playing with the children that gave birth to a sensation which thrilled the ship from end to end. He was trying patiently, persistently, to amuse a little, ailing tot. It was beginning to seem certain that she would not last the voyage out. The mother was in agony as she held the tiny wailing, creature out toward him while he cooed to it and touched its cheek with tender fingers, trying to arouse its interest without success. It was as a final effort to amuse it that he took his flute out of the curious leather case he always carried.

Just as dusk fell on the vessel he began to play.

At first, the strains were soft and low, for the child's benefit, alone, scarce audible at any distance. Almost instantly she quieted, and, as Vanderlyn came up from dinner in the big saloon and glanced across the rail, as usual, he saw a little group of fascinated folk there, close about the flute-player, and faintly heard the sweet, pathetic strains of an old German cradle-song. So soft the sounds were, though, that he could barely catch them, and, therefore, at first, he did not wholly realize their beauty.

Soon, though, the old man plainly utterly forgot the fact that there were other people near than the now quiet child, its mother, his Anna and himself, for he threw more force into his playing. The steerage-passengers drew closer in a reverent silence, as the European peasant always will at sound of really good music, and many of the first-cabin passengers joined John at the rail, attracted by the sweet and soaring melody. In a few moments a full score had gathered there, all listening, intent, enthralled, quite silent.

"Marfellous! He iss a firtuoso!" grumbled a big German at John's side. John turned to him and smiled. The man, he knew, was Anton Karrosch an operatic impresario. He was glad to have his own impression of the wondrous merit of the playing confirmed by an authority.

"He seems to be quite poor," he whispered eagerly. "Perhaps you might find something for him, when we reach New York. He—"

"Ach! He will have no droobles," said Herr Karrosch. "A man who blays like dot! Ven ve land, I see him; yes."

A moment later the flute-player glanced up and saw the audience behind the rail. Instantly he lowered his slim instrument, from whose silver mountings, now, the moonlight was beginning to glint prettily. He gave the prosperous folk above but one short glance, apparently a bit resentful, and then, as if they were of small importance, turned from them to the mother of the child.

"Does she sleep, still?" John could hear him ask, as he bent above the infant.

"Si, si," said the grateful mother, understanding what he meant, although, apparently, she spoke no English.

"Good," said the flute-player, "I stop playing, then." And in spite of a mild spatter of applause from the first-cabin deck and one or two requests for more of his delightful music, he rose and went within. It was clear that his soft courtesies, free performances, were for the poor folk in the steerage, not for the rich upon the promenade.

Mrs. Vanderlyn was, after this, more than ever anxious to have John approach the man and make acquaintance with him; but his belief that such a course would be impertinent was strengthened. What the impresario had said saddened him a little as he reflected on it. He had begun to hope that, when they landed (not before), he might be of service to the pair; but if what Karrosch had said was true, then they would not need his kindnesses. Almost he had made up his mind, thus soon, that the shy little German girl was the one woman in the world for him, so he found it difficult to stop himself from hoping that the fat manager's predictions would prove false; that the flute-player might really find difficulty in arranging a career in the United States; that he, himself, might prove to be essential to the development of his opportunity.

He felt a little gloomy, when, long after most of the ship's company had gone to sleep, he sought his stateroom. Fear that he would find it quite impossible to win his way even to acquaintance, much depressed him.

But the very day the ship turned into the wide beauty of the Lower Bay, a situation grew out of the commonplace of life upon the steerage-deck which sharply and dramatically involved him with the two who had so interested him.

The steerage passengers were dancing to the music of a concertina, many of them, more especially the Italians, joining in the merriment with a gay fervor born of their elation at approach to the rich mysteries of the new land they sought. Much cheap wine had been consumed among them, and in some of them this had, already, wrought its vicious alchemy and changed the gold of sunny tempers into the dross of ugliness. Among those most affected by the liquor was the man Moresco, who so continually boasted of the great things he had done in New York politics and who, since his rebuff by the old German, when he had tried to induce Anna to drink with him, had eyed the pair askance, resentfully.

Young Vanderlyn observed that he was oftener and oftener, as he drank and danced with women of his own race, turning envious and longing eyes toward the beautiful young German girl, throwing resentful, scowling glances at her father, who, on that previous occasion, had so notably rebuffed him. It became quite plain, ere long, that the man had worked up a great wrath against the flute-player.

"I am Pietro Moresco," he boasted, many times, as if the very name should awe the world. Then, impressively: "I am no common emigrant. Not a common emigrant, as all may learn, in time. In New York none are too proud to dance with me. It is not a land for the aristocrat—the aristocrat who travels steerage!"

He gazed at the old man fixedly, with that malevolent look of which none but an Italian really is capable. Vanderlyn saw, also, with amazement, that there were those among his countrymen—men evidently knowing him—who were as much impressed by what he said as, evidently, he believed the whole world ought to be. It almost seemed, indeed, that these folk took his boastings seriously and thought the old man and his daughter really had cause to fear the man's reprisals.

The old man paid no heed to him, however. He only drew his daughter closer to his side. John noted that her cheeks were hotly flushed with anger, combined, perhaps, with fear, and felt the blood of wrath flood to his own and out again, leaving them, he knew, quite ghastly pale. He always flushed, then paled, when he was very angry, and when that pallor clung, as it did now, dire things inevitably impended. He was astonished at the strength of cold resentment in his heart toward the Italian. He did not for an instant hesitate in deciding to protect the little girl from her tormentor, if need arose, at any hazard. It did not once occur to him that this was not his work, that the ship's officers would doubtless maintain order and, themselves, protect her as a matter of mere discipline on board. Indeed, it seemed to him that for some reason the Italian received more than ordinary courtesy from them. As the episode developed, they appeared to edge away, leaving the swarthy bully wholly undisturbed.

He did not fail to take advantage of this situation, but, after glancing somewhat cautiously around, followed his declaration of his own importance and resentment with an angry dive, and, an instant later, had the girl by the right arm, while his countrymen called loudly in approval. Another instant and the man was dragging Anna to the center of the open space where dancing had been going on.

She screamed, her father rose, amazed, resentful, lurching with fierce but futile rage toward their tormentor as the ship rolled, and the slight push which the Italian gave him as he advanced upon him, was all that was required to throw him heavily. Dazed by the fall he lay there, for a moment, helpless, and by the time he rose the girl, shrieking with alarm, was being whirled in the Italian's arms in a crude dance. With a short laugh the man with the accordeon had started up a faster waltz, and there were dozens who, applauding their bold leader, looked on with delight.

But the single spectator above, behind the promenade-deck rail, did not look on with delight. He lost no time. He did not even waste ten seconds in rushing to the little stairway which led downward from his place of vantage, but, with the wiry hand and arm of the trained college athlete to help him in the spring, he vaulted lightly clean across the barrier, and, with legs bent skilfully to break the force of the long drop, landed like a lithe and angry tiger on the deck below, within two feet of the utterly amazed and terrified Moresco.

Once there the young American proceeded neatly, rapidly. Almost instantly the Italian bully was sprawling in the scuppers and Vanderlyn had raised the old man to his feet. In another moment he had taken the girl's hand, led her to her father and they were both trying, in excited German and in English, suffering from the stress of their emotions, to express their thanks to him.

It was at this moment that they met with one of the greatest surprises of their lives. With a sharp cry M'riar burst on them. She had been, as usual, hiding miserably in the narrow entrance to the companion-way which led down to the steerage sleeping quarters, where, daily, since she had in part recovered from her fierce attack of seasickness, she had lurked with furtive eyes and worried heart, squeezing herself against the bulkhead to give others way as they went up or down, afraid to let the voyage end without revealing to her friends her presence, lest they escape to leave her at the mercy of the outraged law of the new land, of which she heard much gossip; afraid to let them know that she was there, lest they, in anger at her presence, refuse to let her join them. But this situation was too much for her. Seeing her adored ones in distress she could restrain herself no longer. She sprang out to the open deck and ranged herself, a veritable little fury, between her friends and the prostrate Italian.

"Garn! Don't yer dare to tech 'er! Garn! Garn!" she cried and poised, tense, vicious, ready to pit her puny strength against his might if he should rise, vanquish Vanderlyn and try, again, to trouble Anna and her father.

But members of the ship's crew now rushed up, and, seemingly almost against their will (Moresco, being in New York City politics, might control much steerage business for the line), but yielding to the loud demand of many passengers above, who, attracted by the shouts, had crowded to the rail, caught the man as, rising, he would have sprung upon the young American. A moment later and he had been dragged away and the blushing rescuer of beauty in distress and old age vanquished, had, stammering in embarrassment before the thanks of his two beneficiaries, gone back to his own part of the ship. He might have wholly lost his self-possession had not the vicious glance of the Italian and a shouted curse come to him while the man was struggling viciously with his unwilling captors. It cheered him unto laughter to hear Moresco laying claim to that mysterious importance which he had so often boasted, and note that he was threatening him with awful things. Much more interesting he found the small scene he was leaving, in which two utterly bewildered and astonished Germans and a little cockney girl were the three actors.

"M'ri-arrr! *M'ri*-arrr!" he heard Anna cry in sheer amazement. "*M'ri*-arrr!"

"Mine Gott im himmel! It is M'ria-arrr!" he heard Kreutzer say.

CHAPTER III

Bartholdi's mighty Liberty loomed high above the vessel as she grandly swept her way among the crowded shipping of the Upper Bay. On the huddled steerage-deck Moresco, quickly and mysteriously free from durance and not at all abashed by what had happened to him, led a little cheering, in which his countrymen joined somewhat faintly. On the promenade-deck Vanderlyn was acting as the leader of enthusiastic rooters for his native land.

With his mother, whose interest in the old German and his daughter he now fostered very eagerly, he stood close by the rail across which he had vaulted when Moresco had assaulted the old man. Not even the enthusiasm of partings from new friends, ship made, could draw him from this point as the vessel neared her dock. From it he watched the workings of the health-and customs-officers among the steerage-passengers, while he tried to definitely decide upon what means he might employ to keep from losing sight of the two people in whom his interest had grown to be so great, after they were diverted by the formalities of immigration laws from the line of travel he would naturally follow when the ship tied up.

"The immigrants are sent to Ellis Island," he explained to Mrs. Vanderlyn. "A case of sheep and goats, all right,

Edward Marshall and Charles T. Dazey

according to the tenets of this land of liberty and lucre. If you've got money you're a sheep. Columbia, the Gem of the Ocean, has wide-open arms for you. No one tries to stop your entrance. If you've none, why you're the goat and everybody butts you."

"Your English is as hard to understand as any of the foreign languages!" his mother chided. "Every other word is slang. I haven't an idea what you mean." Down upon the steerage-deck Moresco, after the faint cheering, was declaiming loudly, now, about the towering statue and the liberty she symbolizes.

Towards the mighty effigy the old flute-player's eyes were also turned, but the emotions it aroused in him were very different from those which the Italian laid his claim to. To him she did not stand for license, but for a freedom from that mysterious worry, which, in London, had been so horridly persistent, which had reached an intolerable climax in Hyde Park, that day when he had run across the German with the turned-up moustache, and from which the journey to America was a veritable flight. The Giant Woman of the Bay would prove to be to him, the old musician fondly hoped, what her designer had intended her to be to all the worried, fleeing people of all the balance of the earth—a great torch-bearer who would light the way to peace and plenty, free from the social and political turmoil and oppression of the worn-out lands across the sea. He drew a breath of crisp air into his lungs, held his daughter closer to his side, took off his hat and stood agaze while the brisk wind, strengthening for the moment, blew the folk around him free of steerage odors, waved his long grey hair about his forehead and flapped his long grey coat about his legs until its tails snapped.

An instant later and combined assaults of manifold officials, pregnant with prying questions and suspicious glances, had driven all thoughts from his mind and those of other steerage passengers that America meant freedom. Never had he been so suddenly and vigorously deluged with such an avalanche of legal interference and investigation. Many a Russian, fleeing here in search of liberty, has been dismayed into concluding that he has but stumbled into a new serfdom, when blue-coats and brass-buttons have descended on him as his ship reached New York Bay.

One arm clasped tight in one of his, the other holding M'riar closely to her side in the dense, swaying crowd, his daughter, as he pondered on these matters, answered questions, worried, was thinking of far different things. Ever since the champion of her cause and her father's against the common enemy, Moresco, had sprung lightly to the steerage-deck from back of the first-cabin rail, her thoughts had been more of that champion than of all other combined details of these most exciting days. Shy and delighted, venturing on new and untried paths they had been, till now; but now, as the long voyage was ending, she was filled with blank dismay. She had heard the talk about the separation of the steerage passengers from the first-cabin passengers, before they landed, and this gave birth to painfully defined convictions that the dream, which, almost without her knowledge, had sprung into being in her heart, must now abruptly end. She would never see her champion again! The thought led on to others, equally disturbing. For the first time in her life her heart was asking questions of her reason.

Who was she? What was she? Why had her father kept her, all her life, in such seclusion? In London she had noted it and wondered at it, but had been content to make no inquiries, because she had not had the wish to go about and do as, from behind the lattice of the close seclusion which confined her, she saw other girls of her age do. She had never had a close friend in her life, except her father, unless one counted M'riar, humble and devoted worshiper, a friend, or unless some memories of bygone days, so faint that they might well be dreams, and which, sometimes, she thought *were* dreams, were truth instead of waking fancies. Vague, they were, and shadowy, including visions of a merry life, as a small tot, in a far country, and a lovely woman who some-times, while propped up with the pillows of a bed, held her to her breast. Then it seemed as if all these delightful things had been brought to an end in one short day. Vaguely she recalled a dreadful time when the great bed on which the lovely woman had reclined was empty.

All that her brain presented in the way of record of the weeks which followed, were, first, a series of dim pictures of a hurried journey, partaking of the nature of a flight from some impending danger. Her father, she remembered, held her almost constantly against his breast, while they were on this journey, so tightly that the clasp of his strong arms was, sometimes, almost painful, and watched continually from carriage windows, from the deck of a small vessel, and, afterwards, from the windows of a railway train, when they paused at stations in the pleasant English country, as if he ever feared that someone would appear to intercept them and carry her away from him. Then her home had been of a kind new to her—the lodging-house. Instead of being in the midst of splendid lawns and mighty trees, she had been hedged about by grimy streets and dull brick buildings; the air which had been all a-sparkle for her in her babyhood, was, through her youth, dull, smoke-grimed, fog-soaked; for roomy spaciousness and gentle luxury had been exchanged the dinginess and squalor of the place in Soho. The occasional visits to the theatre where her father played the flute, now and then a Sunday walk with him when the weather was sufficiently urbane (marred, always, by his peering watch of every passing face, which had never been rewarded till they met the staring stranger in Hyde Park) had been almost the only variations of a dull routine of life, until this journey had begun which had just brought them to the mighty New World harbor. She was vastly puzzled by existence as she stood there in the stuffy crowd and let her mind roam back in retrospect. Her life was all a mystery to her.

This journey was the one tremendous episode of her career; her life in London had been singularly bare of real events; there had only been her daily grind at books which her father wished to have her diligently study, the bi-weekly visits of a woman who had taught her languages and needlework and never talked of anything but youth and romance, although she, herself, was old, and, presumably, beyond the pale of romance. Except for this old woman and the landlady of the cheap lodging-house she had had no friends except poor M'riar.

From such a dull existence, to be thrust into the whirl of this amazing voyage, had been very wonderful, for what might not the new life in the new land mean? Anything, to her young and keen imagination. In this marvelous new country the old Frenchwoman had assured her women were as free as men. What would such freedom bring to her? Riches, possibly, would here reward her father for his artistry upon the flute, and luxuries surround them both, in consequence. And romance! Her heart began to flutter at mere thought of the word, and her mind, against her modest maiden will, involuntarily turned to the youth who had so splendidly sprung to their rescue from the malign Moresco. Ah, how strong, how handsome he had been as he had thrown himself upon the big Italian! She blushed before her own brain's boldness. In that youth undoubtedly might, even now, be found the hero of the romance which the new world would undoubtedly unfold for her delighted eyes to read! Singularly innocent and ignorant of many things which most girls of her age know well, she did not stop to reason any of this out—she merely felt the firm conviction of its certainty, and, for a time, was glad.

But as the ship passed slowly up the river, and, finally, was taken charge of by the grimy tugs which nosed her with much labor into place at a great dock, the officers began to hustle all the steerage passengers into more compact masses on the deck and her attention once more centered on the matters of the moment. The building on the dock shut off the free salt breeze and quickly the unclean breath of the crowd distressed her lungs. The worried immigrants trod on one another's heels, fell across their huddled trunks and bundles, chattered, gayly or in fright, close in each other's ears. There was a long delay, in which, if one of the poor throng dared move beyond the boundaries set for them by the burly officers in charge, loud language, not too nice to hear, was the result, and, even, once or twice, a blow. She heard an English-speaking veteran of many voyages explaining to his uncomfortable fellows what Vanderlyn had told his mother about them: that because they had come in the steerage they could not land upon the dock, as did the passengers of the first-cabin, but would be borne to some far spot for further health-inspection and examination as to their ability to earn their livelihoods.

This worried her, as it had Vanderlyn. Suppose her father should not satisfy these stern examiners? Would the authorities consider that ability to play a flute divinely was sufficient ground for thinking that a man could earn his way? And, if they were landed in two different places, how would the young man know just where to look for her? She almost paled at thought that, possibly, she might be whisked beyond his ken; but then there came the thought of his ability in an emergency, as evidenced by his flying leap down to her rescue, and, shyly smiling, she comforted herself with the reflection that that wondrous youth could make no failures. That he thought of her she could not doubt, for she had never missed one of his frank, admiring glances, although, apparently, she had missed most of them. She finally became quite sure he would not lose sight of her, and this was comforting.

For a full hour, after the ship had tied up to her dock, all on that deck were forced to stand in stuffy quarters, odorous and almost dark. Between Anna and her father huddled M'riar, frightened, now, and snuffling, clinging desperately to the hand of the loved mistress she had run away to serve. The flute-player, almost fainting from the heat and weariness, strove bravely to conceal this from his daughter, and, with pitiful assumption of fine strength, smiled down at her, through the thick gloom, from time to time, with reassurance, attempting to instill in her a courage which he, himself, she plainly saw, was losing rapidly.

Clearly some of his oldtime worry had returned to him. It might be, he was reflecting, that this far America was not as far as he had thought, and that he stood as much chance of encountering that danger which had made him fly from London, as he had stood there! This troubled her intensely.

The odors of that crowded steerage gangway, the pressing of the weary women, the wailing of the frightened babies, the cursing of the men, as time passed, made the place seem an inferno. M'riar, weak from seasickness, terrified by conversation which she heard around her about the deportation of such immigrants as had no money or too little, and fearful that she might be torn from the dear side of her beloved mistress in spite of all which she had done to follow her, shivered constantly and sometimes shook with a dry sob. The hours were hours of nightmare.

Many of the women were half-fainting when, at last, the barges of the government were drawn up at the ship's side for the transfer of the immigrants to Ellis Island, and across the narrow planks which stretched from them to the dingy little liner the motley crowd trooped wearily. Kreutzer was near to absolute exhaustion, and shouldered their heavy trunk, lifted their heaviest bag, with difficulty. His knees, it seemed to him, must certainly give way beneath him. Seeing this gave M'riar something other than her fears to think of.

"Gimme th' bag, now, guvnor," she said quietly, although both she and Anna already were well burdened.

"Nein," said the old man, gravely. "Child, you could not carry it."

"*I* could," said Anna, quickly, and tried to take it from his hand, abashed that the small servant should have been more thoughtful of him than she was.

"Not much yer cawn't," said M'riar, positively. "I 'yn't goin' ter let yer, miss. Ketch me! *Me* let yer carry *bags*! My heye!"

"But M'riarrr," Anna answered. "You are so very little and it iss so very big!"

"Carry ten of 'em," said M'riar, nonchalantly and nobly rose to the occasion despite the protests of both Anna and the flute-player.

There was little time for argument, for, an instant later, they were forced forward irresistibly by the pressure of the crowd behind them and soon found themselves, to their inexpressible relief, in the clear air of an open-sided deck on one of the big barges. In another quarter of an hour they had started on their little voyage to the landing station upon Ellis

Island, where Uncle Sam decides upon the fitness of such applicants for admission to his domain as have reached his shores "third-class."

The ordeal at Ellis Island was less formidable, for Kreutzer and his daughter, than the gossip of the steerage had led them to expect. Both were in good health, he had the money which the law requires each immigrant to bring with him, letters avowed his full ability to make a living for himself and daughter, he had not come over under contract. But poor M'riar! Her skinny little form, weak eyes, flat chest, barely passed the medical examination; Herr Kreutzer did not understand some of the questions put to her and thus she nearly went on record as being without friends or means of winning her support. Indeed he did not realize the situation until a uniformed official had begun to lead the screaming child away and then he made things worse by letting his rare German temper rise as he protested. Had not Anna laid restraining fingers on his arm he might have found himself charged with a serious offense, upon the very threshold of the new land he had journeyed to.

They now formed a thoroughly dismayed, disheartened group of three there under the high, girdered roof of Uncle Sam's reception chamber for prospective children by adoption. Anna, alarmed for both the threatened child and angry flute-player, stood, woefully distressed between the two, a hand upon the arm of each and big, alarmed and wondrously appealing eyes fixed on the gruff official, who stirred uneasily beneath the power of their petition; Kreutzer was frightened, also, now that his wrath was passing and he took time to reflect that if he should involve himself with this new government inquiries would certainly be started which would result in the revelation of his whereabouts to those whom he had hoped utterly to evade; M'riar, the cause of all the trouble, wept like a Niobe, quite soundlessly, shaking like an aspen, managing to maintain her weight upon her weakening knees with desperate effort only.

"Sorry, Miss," said the official, with gruff kindness. "But law's law, you know, and she's against it."

"Little M'riarrr is against your laws?" said Anna, much surprised.

"She's likely to become a public charge," the man said, anxious to defend himself and his government before the lovely girl. "We've got enough of European paupers to support, here in this country, now."

"But she would live with us," said Anna.

"Sure—until you fired her," said the man with a short laugh.

"Firrred her?" Anna said, inquiringly, not guessing at his meaning. "Firrred her? We should be very kind to her. We would not burn her, hurt her in the slightes' way. I promise, sir; I promise."

The official laughed again. "Oh, that's all right, Miss," he explained. "I know you wouldn't hurt her. That ain't what I meant. I meant until you let her go, discharged her, turned her off, decided that you didn't need her help around the house, found somebody who'd work better for you for less money, or something of that sort. She'd never get another job. She's too skinny and too ignorant."

"Hi'll fat up, 'ere, Hi swears Hi will," Maria interrupted hopefully. "Hi'm *certain* to fat up."

"Yes, yes," said Anna, "I am certain that she will be very fat. She will not have so much to do and will have much to eat.

She shall fat up at once." She spoke with honest earnestness. Could leanness be against the law, too, here?

And M'riar, also, had understood exactly what he meant when he had said she was too ignorant. "An' Hi'm that quick to learn!" she said. "You cawn't himagine! W'y, 'yn't Hi halmost learnt me letters off from bundle carts an' 'oardings? M, he, hay, t—that spells 'beef.' The bobby on hour beat, 'e told me, an' Hi 'yn't fergot a mite. T, haych, he, hay, t, r, he, spells 'show.' 'E told me that, too. Hi 'yn't one as would *st'y* hignorant, Hi 'yn't."

"Fer Gawd's sake!" said the officer, entirely nonplussed by this display of the girl's erudition. "Say—well—now—come here, Bill!" He beckoned to another man in blue and shiny buttons. "Spell them words ag'in, Miss, won't you?" he implored.

Anna looked at him reproachfully. "No, no," she said, and made him feel ashamed with her big eyes, "please, sir, not. It is not funny—not for us. Please, please do not send our M'riarrr back to England. It was her love which brought her with us. Real love. You would not punish any one for being truly loving, eh?"

Subdued and made, again, uneasy by her lovely eyes, the man did not complete the exposition of the joke to the newcomer, but took refuge in an attitude of most regretful, but impregnable officialism. "I ain't got a word to say about it, Miss," he hurried to assure the eyes. "Law's law, and law says that the likes of her has got to be sent back. The only way that you could keep her here would be to put up bonds to guarantee th' gover'ment against her goin' on th' town or anything like that."

She did not understand him in the least. "What is it that you mean?" she asked.

Laboriously he made things clear to her, Herr Kreutzer helping and coming to an understanding just before she did.

"Ach!" said the old flute-player, "We cannot. We have not so much."

"Sure. I know that," the man replied. "That is why I say th' girl has got to be sent back."

Argument proved unavailing, and, ten minutes later, poor M'riar, screaming as if red-hot irons were begrilling her most tender spots, was being led into the "pen."

"We'll keep her here a while," the man explained, as he endeavored to avoid the child's astonishingly skilful and astonishingly painful kicks. "Maybe you can find somebody to go bond for her. There ain't no other way. There really ain't, Miss."

During all this speech he still was under the strong influence of Anna's wondrous eyes, else he would never have been able to articulate with such unruffled calm. His charge was doing agonizing things to his official shins, and even pinching him just over the short ribs on his left side with a forefinger and a thumb which showed amazing strength and malice quite infernal.

Anna and her father turned away, perforce, to attend to their own business, after having promised M'riar that they would never let her be sent back; that they would come and take her from the pen tomorrow. Neither had the least idea of a way in which to make this possible, but both swore in their hearts that it should be accomplished.

"Ach!" said Anna, "if only he had traveled in the third class, too! He then would have been with us and would never have permitted it."

"But who, mine liebschen?"

Anna, realizing what she had been saying, colored vividly, but never in her life had she deceived her father, hidden anything from him, or in the slightest way evaded with him, so she summoned courage and said softly: "Why, the—the young gentleman."

"What gentleman?"

"The one on the ship who sprang down when that wicked man caught me to dance with him."

Herr Kreutzer slowly nodded, seeing no significance in her quick thought of Vanderlyn, save that the thought was rare good sense. Being an American, the young man naturally would have been better able to explain the matter to the officers, and, had the matter been enough explained, he thought, they could not, possibly, have had the heart to hold the child. "Ach, yes," said he. "If he was here! He certainly would know."

Luck, that day, as usually in his wealth-smoothed life, was with young Vanderlyn, for, just as Anna and her father were regretting that he was not there, lo, he appeared! It had been through his bull-dog persistence that the elder Vanderlyn had won the wealth which son and wife were spending now, since he had passed on to a shore where wealth of gold may not be freighted. That same bull-dog persistence had the son applied to the momentous problem which confronted him. Not only had he won his difficult mother over to a friendly interest in the lovely German girl who had so utterly enthralled him, but he had made her eager to keep track of her, see more of her. Thus had he readily been freed from the small services which a mother might expect of her grown son on landing day; not only freed, but urged to go upon the search for which his heart craved avidly.

He had had some difficulty in obtaining, quickly, an official permit to repair to Ellis Island, but an opened pocketbook had solved it, in due course of time, and, now, here he was, trying to "frame up," as he expressed it to himself, "some really fair reason for having followed these whom he was seeking."

The excitement of poor M'riar's sad predicament made it unnecessary for him to present the reason which he had, with careful pains at length devised. Kind Fate had wondrously well timed his eager coming.

"What seems to be the trouble?" he asked easily, as he hurried forward with his hat in hand, much comforted by seeing that there was a trouble of some sort.

The matter was explained to him.

"That's easy," he said gaily. "Let me fix it;" and, forthwith, the thing was fixed. Without the slightest hesitation he made himself responsible for M'riar in every way which an ingenious government had managed to devise through years of effort.

The gratitude of the three travelers was earnest and was volubly expressed in spite of his determined efforts to prevent them from expressing it. M'riar would have thrown her arms about his neck and kissed him had not Anna thoughtfully prevented it, after one quick glance at the astonishing appearance of the delighted child's tear-and lunch-stained face.

And so it came about that the Herr Kreutzer and his daughter Anna, with her humble slave and worshiper, M'riar, were ferried back from Ellis Island to New York within a half-a-dozen hours of the moment when they landed on it. As they went Moresco, himself, apparently a citizen, and free to go at once, was still there in the building, working with his boasted "pull" to help his countrymen. He shook his fist at them as they departed and cried insults after them. Few immigrants have ever been passed through in briefer time than was the flute-player; few government inspectors at the landing station have ever been enabled, by a stroke of good luck from a cloudless sky, to take home to their wives, at night, as large a roll of crisp, new money (yellow-backed) as an inspector took home to his wife that night.

"Gee, Bill!" the wife exclaimed when she had finished choking. "When do you expect the cops?"

"What cops?" he naturally asked.

"Them that'll come to pinch you for bank-robbery," she answered, fondling the certificates with reverent, delighted fingers.

An episode of their return from Ellis Island to Manhattan much puzzled Vanderlyn. Puffing and blowing from his hurry (which had been less adroit than Vanderlyn's) they met Karrosch on the New York pier, about to start in search of Kreutzer.

"Ah," he said cordially, "I wish to talk with you. I have the largest orchestra in all America and wish to offer you the place of my first flute. You are very lucky to have had me on the ship with you. I shall be glad to pay—"

Kreutzer interrupted him with courteous shaking of the head. "I thank you, sir," he said, with firm decision. "I cannot play first flute in your large orchestra."

"But," said the astonished Karrosch, "I will pay—"

"I much regret," said Kreutzer, "that I cannot play first flute in your large orchestra."

Vanderlyn, not less than Karrosch, was bewildered by this episode. Only Anna was not in the least surprised by it, although she did not understand it. She knew that he had many times refused alluring offers of the sort in London, always without an explanation of his reasons for so doing.

In the little rooms which they had found for temporary lodging place, Herr Kreutzer sat that evening, with a well-cleaned M'riar standing by and trying to devise some way of adding to his comfort. He had never given much thought to the child, before, he realized; he had accepted her as one of many facts of small importance. Now, though, he noted the devoted gaze with which her eyes were following Anna as she moved about the room, arranging little things.

"You love her, eh?" he asked.

"*Love* 'er!" said M'riar, breathlessly. "My heye! Love *'er*! Ou, Hi, sye!"

Herr Kreutzer reached an arm out with a thrill of real affection and drew the little waif close to him. Never in her life had she been offered a caress, before, by anyone but Anna. It took her by surprise, and, without the slightest thought of doing so, she burst into a flood of tears. He did not fail to understand the workings of her soul. He drew the tiny creature to him and softly pressed a kiss upon her perfectly clean forehead.

"You vould not want to leave her, M'riar?"

"Hi'd die, Hi would," sobbed M'riar.

Herr Kreutzer held her head back and smiled into her eyes with a good smile which made her very happy. "Ach, liebling, do not worry."

"W'y wouldn't yer go with the toff and pl'y in ther big horchestra?" she made bold to ask. "You'd set 'em *cryzy*, you would! *My* 'art turns somersets, it does, w'en you pl'ys on yer flute."

He pushed the child away, almost as if she angered him; then, seeing her remorseful, frightened look, he took her back again and held her close beside his knee.

"I have no love for crowds, my M'riar," he said slowly. "No; not even in America. I have no love for crowds."

CHAPTER IV

Herr Kreutzer's little stock of money (depleted sadly by dishonest exchange) sagged heavily in a small leather bag which he carried in a carefully buttoned hip-pocket in his trousers. There it gave him comfort, as, the day after he had landed in New York, it chinked and thumped against him as he walked. There was so much of it! In this land of gold and generous appreciation of ability, it would be far more than enough to carry him and the two girls who were now dependent on him until he should find a well paid, but not too conspicuous, situation. He was sure of this. It had been the gossip of the little orchestra in London that musicians, in New York, if worthy, were always in demand; that when they played they were paid vastly. Tales often had been told of money literally thrown to players by delighted members of appreciative audiences—money in great rolls of bank-notes, heavy gold-pieces, bank checks. Nowhere in the world, not even in the music loving Fatherland, a wandering trombonist who had visited the states had solemnly assured him, were expert performers on any sort of instrument so well paid and so well beloved as in the city of New York.

"You, Kreutzer," this man had said (for when musicians lie the cultivated and exotic fancy, essential to success in their profession, makes them lie superbly) "could, past the shadow of a doubt, win a real fortune in a season in New York."

"Much work is waiting, eh?" said Kreutzer, eagerly. He did not wish to win a fortune, for that would mean the larger orchestras, but he wondered if the smaller organizations paid proportionally well.

"For such as you," the man replied, maliciously—he was a disappointed, vicious person—"there ever is demand from large and small."

"Why, then, did you come back to England?" the flute-player inquired.

"I? Oh, I am not an artist—a real artist, as you are," was the answer, flattering and vicious. The man had tried to get an introduction to fair Anna and had been refused peremptorily, as all had been refused. He planned to have revenge for it. "The man who merely plays is not so vastly better off, there in the states, than here; but to the *artist*—to the real artist, such as you—the states will literally pay anything."

That the man who had found failure was not a real musician Kreutzer knew. Too often had his trombone trespassed, with its brazen bray, upon the time which the composer had allotted to the soft, delightful flute, to leave the slightest doubt of its performer's rank incompetence. That he had failed was, therefore, easily understood; in no way did it indicate that all he said about the chances of a real musician in the land of skyscrapers and mighty distances (which he also told about at length) was of necessity untrue. It had been the talk of this man which had fascinated Kreutzer; it was the city of this man's wild fancy which the flute-player expected to encounter when he reached New York.

The disillusionment came slowly at the start. Certainly the skyscrapers were existent in a number and a grandeur which the man had not been able to exaggerate; certainly the railway trains ran up and down on iron stilts as he had said they did; certainly the crowds were mighty and amazing both in their brutality and their good nature, just as he had said they were. Many things there were which, for a time, preserved the innocent flute-player's faith in his informant. But when he came to look for work—ah, then vanished the first bubble. Seemingly there was no place in all the city for an old performer on the flute save that which Karrosch offered and which Kreutzer would not take.

Even in this new land, far from those he would avoid, the old flute-player was determined not to go to the great orchestras, among whose auditors were likely to be travelers. Thus he barred himself from opera-houses, theatres and most of the hotels, by the towering barrier of his own timidity. Nor did he wish to join a union (this shut him out from many smaller orchestras) or even to enroll himself at the employment agencies. He would not risk unwelcome prominence even to that slight extent. Instead of doing these things, which would at once have won him profitable work, he tramped the streets, looking for various employment, at first with a resilient hope, then with a careful industry, at the end of the first month with dogged determination, finally with a desperation bordering upon despair.

And there were other things to worry him. Early in his search for work he had made a noontime pause, one day, in a quaint lager-beer saloon much frequented by musicians. There, at the table where he sat, he had encountered one who earnestly announced himself as a "wise guy" and told him much about New York, all quite as pessimistic as the London romancer's talk had been enthusiastic. He suffered from misfortune which he blamed, unhesitatingly, to the vileness of the prosperous and ranted endlessly without attracting much attention till he touched upon the subject of the viciousness of the American rich man with women. This roused Kreutzer fully, for one of the tales the babbler told was of a gilded youth who had befriended poverty in order to obtain the confidence of lowly beauty and then, of course, abused the confidence.

Herr Kreutzer's heart beat madly before the man had finished speaking. Could it be possible that all Americans were of this ilk, as the disgruntled one maintained? If so, then Vanderlyn —ah, it could not be possible! The youth had been too kind to them during the few days of his stay in New York city, before he had departed for the west on a short trip; had promised too much kindness to be offered upon his return! But—Anna!

And so, that very night, he searched until he found another tenement, and, with his own hands, moved their scanty household goods to it, leaving behind him no address. Naturally a sweet and unsuspicious soul, he had never dreamed of treachery upon the part of the ingratiating youth; now suspicion's seeds were sown in his old mind and fertilized by rising tears of disillusionment in most things which he had found in New York, he was ready to be doubtful of the most undoubtable.

The new quarters were much less desirable, in every way, than those they had abandoned, and the rent was higher; but they were quite the best the old man could discover on short notice, and quite the lowest priced. He never dreamed, as he argued with his new landlord over rent that the old rental had been cut almost in half to him because young Vanderlyn had made arrangements surreptitiously. He entered the new tenement with the firm conviction that he had been swindled in the rent which he had paid, "cash in advance," and, that night, was very gloomy.

So, also, were the bewildered Anna and M'riar.

Edward Marshall and Charles T. Dazey

"Hi sye, Miss," said M'riar, when they were alone, while the flute-player went out for the supper, "wot'll that young toff think, comin' back an' findin' yer gone orf from there?"

"Surely there was left behind the address of this place," said Anna, with small confidence of this in her own heart.

"Hi 'eard the lawst word said," said M'riar, with conviction, "an' hall yer farther told th' geezer was that 'e was goin' to quit."

"But, he would not possibly be so lacking in his courtesy! He—"

Just then the flute-player returned and Anna asked him, boldly, but with a studied air of carelessness, about the matter. It was the first time in her whole life that she had ever tried to hide her real emotions from her father.

"Leave our address for Herr Vanderlyn?" said Kreutzer, who had been waiting for the question and had schooled himself to answer it without revealing the real facts. "Of course. Of course. Why not?" It was the first time he had ever actually lied to Anna. Things, thus, were in a bad way at the start in the new quarters.

M'riar, after the first day there, did the marketing. The streets, transformed into deep, narrow canons by the towering buildings bordering them, swarming with the poor of every nationality on earth, every block made into a most fascinating market by the push-cart vendors with their varied wares, had, from the start, enthralled her. She was uncannily acute at bargaining. Soon more than one red-headed Jew had learned, in self-defense, to take out the stick which held up one end of his cart, and move along, at sight of her. Too often she had been the symbol of financial loss. Her "Hi sye!" and "My heye!" became the keen delight of German maidens back of counters over which cheap delicatessen was distributed.

Beyond a doubt M'riar was in her element. She labored day and night. Few tasks there were about the tiny three-room menage, save the actual cooking, which she did not undertake and undertake with energy which made up, largely, for her lack of skill. Herr Kreutzer, who had been in doubt about the wisdom of engrafting her upon his little family looked at her with amazement, sometimes lowering his flute, on which he might be practicing, in the very middle of a bar, so that he might better stare at her unbounded and unceasing physical activities. She abandoned, as unworthy of her mistress, her old form of address and no longer simply called her "Miss," but "Frow-*line*," after tutelage from the small shop-woman who sold cheese to her in three-cent packages.

But, ere much time had passed, the day arrived when Herr Kreutzer feared to have her even buy so much of luxury as cheese in three-cent packages. The little bag of money which had chinked so bravely on his hip when he had first arrived in New York city scarcely chinked at all, these days. Everything was so expensive in this new land they had come to! Not only must he pay as much rent for a three-room tenement, with one room almost dark and one quite windowless, as he had had to pay, in London, for the comfortable floor which they had occupied in Soho, but food cost twice as much, he woefully declared—and played the "Miserere" on his flute. He would not go to Karrosch, or any of the large, important orchestras; none of the small ones wished a flutist. He learned to loathe the mere word "phonograph"—in so many places did it form a clock-work substitute to do the work he longed to do.

It was when want actually stared them in the face that he

read an advertisement in a German newspaper for a musician —flute or clarinet—in a beer garden. The clock-hands had not yet reached eight when he presented himself at the address, far uptown. He had been unsuccessful, once or twice, in getting hearings because he had arrived too late— these days he rose by four and had a paper fresh and damp from the great presses, and every advertisement in it read by five o'clock.

There were many applicants for the position, and by ten o'clock when a youth with a red face and a hoarse voice appeared behind the wicket at the side of the main entrance, peered out curiously at the shabby, anxious crowd and winked derisively before he let the door swing inwards, Herr Kreutzer was as weary as he well could be and keep upright upon his feet; but, notwithstanding this, he had not given ground and still held first place in the line. He had arrived at a decision which filled his soul with dread. If he failed to get this place he would apply to one of the great orchestras! This possibility he thought of with a desperate dismay, for, playing thus before the prosperous public, some traveler would be sure to see him, recognize him, send word back to Germany and then—ah, then the deluge! He had been sadly disappointed when he had discovered that New York is not remote from Europe, but as cosmopolitan, almost, as London. Here, as there, asylum only could be found in the remote resorts, unfrequented by those with means, by travelers, by those who know good music. Ah! he shuddered at the thought of what might happen if, some night, forgetting his surroundings, he should play as he *could* play in hearing of a connoisseur. Then, certainly, discovery.

So he was very anxious to obtain this small position in the little, far beer-garden. He was sorry for the others, but they could not have necessities the least bit greater than his own. He must not yield to them, so, in the eager crowd, he pushed and scrambled as the others did, and always kept in front.

"What kin yer play?" the fat and blear-eyed manager asked gruffly.

"I play the flute."

"Bring it along?"

"Yah; surely."

"Let 'er go, then. Give us something good and lively."

With nervous hands Herr Kreutzer raised the old flute to his lips, with fingers which put tremolos where none were written in the score; but he made many of the notes dance joyously. Through anxious lips he blew his soul into the instrument—his love of the pre-eminent composer who had sung the song he played, his love of his sweet daughter for whose sake he played—his love of her and fear for her if he should fail to win the favor of his burly listener. The great "Spring Song" of Mendelssohn has never been played on a flute as Kreutzer played it, in the grey light of that morning in the cheerless, bare beer-garden. When he had finished there was silence in the crowd behind him. Not a man among the applicants for the position was a real musician, but all knew, instinctively, that they had been listening to a veritable artist. Then, after an awed moment, there came a little spatter of applause. All these men were seeking for a chance to earn the mere necessities of life; every one of them was more than anxious, was pitifully eager for the small position which was open; but, having heard Herr Kreutzer play, they hoped no longer—and were generous.

The owner of the beer-garden looked on them in surprise.

"Got it all framed up," he said, "that Dutchy is to have the job, have you?" He turned, then, to Kreutzer. "That's all right, too, I guess. Showed you can play real fast and that is somethin' with a crowd, all right, all right. But don't you know some really *good* music?"

"Good music!" Kreutzer faltered, at a loss. That which he had played had been among the best the world has ever known.

"Yes; rag-time stuff, an' such. Real pop'lar."

"No," said Kreutzer, sadly, "I fear I do not know good music of the kind you name." He made as if to turn away, but then bethought himself and whirled back hopefully. "But I can learn," he said. "Simple things, without a doubt, I could play on sight."

"Off the notes, you mean?"

"Yah; so."

"Take this, then." The manager held toward him a thick book of rag-time melodies.

Kreutzer, too desperate to be disgusted, ran through half-a-dozen of them rapidly. Now the manager beamed pleasantly.

"Say, you'll do, all right, all right," he told the flute-player. Then, turning to the rest he motioned them away. "Beat it, you guys," he commanded. "Father Rhine here's got the job."

CHAPTER V

Down in the new tenement Anna and her little slave, M'riar, worked hard, that day, at cleaning.

"W'ere Hi wuz born," M'riar gravely commented, "we wuz brought up on dirt an' liked hit, but we never wusn't greedy for hit, like th' way these folks, 'ere, 'as been."

Anna, in the next room, was for the first time in her life working with a scrubbing-brush, and, presently, M'riar heard its swish.

"Hi s'y!" she cried, and dashed into the gloomy cubby-hole. "Wot's this? You scrubbin'? Drop it, now, you 'ear? Hit 'yn't fer me to show no disrespeck, Frow*line*, but—drop it. Hi 'yn't a-goin' to have them pretty 'ands hall spoilt."

"But, M'riarrr, I just *love* to scrub."

"Don't love hanythink so vulgar," M'riar replied without a moment's hesitation. "Don't *you* bother lovin' hanythink but just the guvnor, and—and—Mr. Vanderlyn." She looked down at blushing Anna who, upon her knees, was astonished almost into full paralysis. And then she shrilly laughed.

"*Hi* knows!" said she. "*Hi* knows."

"M'riarrr," said Anna slowly, rising, "you are crrazy."

"Not so cryzy as a 'ackman 'ammerin' 'is 'ead hagainst a 'ouse." said M'riar. "There's cryzier. Love mykes 'em that w'y."

"Quite crrazy," Anna answered; but she was blushing furiously.

"Blushin' red as beefstykes," M'riar commented as she took the brush and started to do Anna's painfully accomplished task all over, from the big crack by the door where she had started. "'Ow's 'e hever goin' to know w'ere we 'ave moved to?" she asked her mistress, now.

"Father left a word."

"Ho, did 'e?" M'riar asked.

"Yes; certainly."

"Ho, *did* 'e!" M'riar exclaimed again. "Wot mykes yer think 'e did?"

"He told me so."

M'riar sat back, astounded. She knew he had not done so, for she, herself, had asked the landlord there and been assured that no hint had been given. She did not know just what to do, but soon reached a decision.

"Hi'll tell yer, frow-line. I reckon 'e forgot or else th' toff there, 'e don't ricollick. Hi knows as 'e don't know w'ere 'tis we've come to. 'E tol' me hit 'ad slipped 'is mind."

"Oh," said Anna, in distress.

"'Ow's Mr. Vanderlyn to find, then?"

"Oh, I do not know," said Anna in dismay.

"Hi do," said M'riar, scrubbing furiously toward Anna till that dainty maiden fled before her and took refuge in the doorway. "Hi'm goin' back there to leave word fer 'im."

"Father might not wish—" Anna began doubtfully.

"Mr. Vanderlyn—'e would," said M'riar.

"Perhaps—he might," said Anna.

When Herr Kreutzer reached the tenement again he was both humbled and elated. To have discovered any kind of work was fortunate, to have found the only place available a cheap beer-garden was disheartening. But work he had and they could live, which surely was a great deal to be thankful for.

"Ach, liebschen," he exclaimed on entering, anxious to apprise her of his luck, loath to tell her all its details. "I have work. I play first flute, from this time onwards, in a— pleasure park." He did not tell her that there was no second flute or any other instrument save a terrible piano, played by a black "professor"; he did not tell her that "the park" was a beer-garden.

She rushed to him and threw her arms about his neck.

"We celebrate a little," he said grandly, and began to draw out of his great-coat pockets the materials for a bona-fide dinner, for, knowing that he could redeem it the next Saturday, he had put his watch in pawn. They had not had real dinners lately. "M'riar, she will cook it."

"My heye!" said M'riar, taking the first package, and, when he followed it with others: "Ho, Hi sye!"

She had just come in from her uncannily quick dash across town—M'riar had learned the simple key to New York's streets and rushed about them without fear—to leave their new address for Mr. Vanderlyn. She felt, therefore, that she had accomplished a good deed that day and was in the very highest spirits. She went to work upon the supper with a will and singing, which greatly distressed Kreutzer, although he would not have expressed his pain for worlds.

"I work from six to eleven," he told his daughter, in explaining the arrangement he had made. The manager had said that at eleven all sober folks had gone and that those who still remained were all too drunk to know if there was music or was not; but the old man did not tell his daughter this. He hoped that she would never know how humble and unpleasant the work which he had found must be.

The very next day Vanderlyn appeared, to M'riar's satis-faction and Anna's fluttering joy. He was most respectful, plainly very anxious to be of further service to her and her father. She felt a little guilty because she had sent M'riar with the address—if her father had not left it he certainly had failed to for no other purpose than preventing Vanderlyn from getting it—but surely it was right for her to be good friends with one who wished to be so kind to him and her! An hour passed most delightfully in that earnest conversation about little which engages young folk of their age and suffering from the complaint which ailed them both.

"But I really had a solemn, sober errand to attend to when I came," he said, at length. "My mother fell in love with you." (He wished he might have told her that her son had, also.) "She is anxious to see more of you." (He did not tell her that the reason was his mother's firm conviction that her father certainly was a distinguished person in hard luck, incog.) "This summer, while she was in Europe, she found that she was sadly handicapped by knowing almost nothing of the German language. She wants to know if you won't come to her and teach her. You could also be her friend, you know; a sort of young companion to a lonely woman." He was making it sound as attractive as he could. He had devised the scheme with earnest care, had brought his mother round to eagerness for it with cautious difficulty, and now presented it with diffidence and fear to the delightful girl he loved.

"I teach?" said Anna, delighted by the thought of being able, thus, to help her father, and, at the same time, not utterly averse to anything which would make frequent glimpses of her knight-errant an easy certainty. "I don't know if I *could* teach."

"Why, it's a cinch," said the enthusiastic lover. "I don't think she will be slow to learn. She'll work hard, mother will; she didn't like this summer's trip too well. The crowned-heads didn't tip their crowns and bow as she went by."

"You are mistake," said Anna gravely. "Kings do not wear their crowns upon the streets."

He laughed. "You see how much we've got to learn?" he asked. "May I tell my mother that you'll come?"

"I shall ask my father," Anna answered.

Reluctantly, after a week, Herr Kreutzer gave consent. He was afraid he might not hold the place in the beer-garden. He hated the cheap rag-time music which the man insisted on and had held his temper with much difficulty, when he had been reproved for playing "hymns" because he had, for solos, interspersed a worthy number now and then. With his tenure of that place uncertain, not sure that he could find another, he felt that he would have no right to interpose too serious objections to the highly flattering arrangement Mrs. Vanderlyn proposed. His worry about Vanderlyn subsided, somewhat, when he found the young man was away from town much of the time.

The little tenement-house apartment was a lonely place, when he was there, after Anna took up her new work and could come to it but once a week and M'riar was a comfort to him. An astonishing companionship grew up between the strangely differing pair. To save his ears he taught her something about singing; to save her pride from gibings from the other children in the block (who were irreverent and sometimes made a little fun of Kreutzer) she saw to it that he was always brushed when he went out. Indeed she made him very comfortable.

Monday afternoons were what made life worth living, though, to him. On Monday afternoons there was no music at the beer-garden and Mrs. Vanderlyn gave Anna, also, that time to herself so they had these hours together, reunited.

Anna's absence from him among strangers was a constant worry and humiliation to him. He reproached himself continually because his poverty had made it necessary. She was at that age, he knew, when maidens learn to love, and she must never learn to love until—until he could go back, with her to his dear Germany, where were such men as he would choose for her. And when would that be safe? Oh, when would that be safe!

He wondered if it was not yet time to trust her with the secret which he had concealed from her her whole life long. The temptation was tremendous. Some day she would know why he had lived, must live a fugitive. Must he wait on, for other weary years? He sat immersed in thought of these things, while M'riar worked at making everything as near to neat perfection as her training in the London lodging-house made possible.

The old man's thoughts dwelt much upon young Vanderlyn. His Anna would see much of him, ere long, when the young man's western trips were ended. But she must not fall in love with him! It would not do for Anna Kreutzer, daughter of the beer-garden flute-player, to marry an American. But how, without revealing to her what he hid, could he be certain that she understood this? He wondered if it had not been a great mistake to let her go to Mrs. Vanderlyn, and then laughed bitterly because he had not "let" her go; a grim necessity had forced it—it, or something else which might have been much less desirable.

It was almost dinner-time when Anna came—radiantly beautiful, with her crisp color heightened by the rapid run from her employer's in the Vanderlyn's great touring-car. She had not wished to ride in it, but had been told to, so that she might have the time to do some errands and still get to her home on time.

"It is fine for you, up there, at the great house of Mrs. Vanderlyn, eh, Anna?" said the old man after they had greeted one another lovingly.

"But yes," said Anna, "it is pleasant. She is kind—oh, ve-ry kind; but, father, I miss you! I miss you every day and every hour. Of mornings, when I rise, I wonder what it is that you are having, down here in the little home, for breakfast. I wonder if M'riarrr still is thoughtful and remembers all that she has learned about the sweeping and the scrrrubbing. I wonder how things went with you the night before, in that grreat orchestra at that amusement park. Do they still think the first-flute a gr-r-reat musician, father?"

He smiled. "At the garden none has, so far, made complaint about my playing," he said slowly, "except that I am not quite willing, sometimes, to play the music they seem best to like." He would not have told her all the details of his battles against rag-time, for the world. "It is music of the negroes, Anna. Er—er—syncopation. Ach! *What* syncopation! All right in its place, my dear, but a whole evening of it! Ach, drives me—it grows tiresome, Anna."

"Some day, father, you will not play there," she said with emphasis. "Some day will come fortune to us—some day."

"Yes; perhaps; some day. But there is something finer than a fortune, Anna. I have been thinking, thinking, thinking, lately, of your mother, Anna. How delighted she would be to see you, now, with your dark hair! Why, Anna, it is almost black! So delighted she would be! It was blonde when you were born—blonde, fair like mine, before mine turned to white; but hers was dark, as yours is now, and I think that when she saw that yours was light she was a little disappointed till her old nurse told her that in early years her own hair had been as yours was. You were one year old, my Anna, before your hair began to show the brown."

"Do you like it, father?"

"Like it? Ah, I love it! But—I am worried."

"Worried?"

"Yes. Always in the past have I been with you. Now you are alone and beautiful. And of life you know so little, while of love—you know—ah, nothing!"

Anna was not sure of this. She had been wondering, indeed, if she did not know much of it. It startled her to have her father speak of it. There had been tremors in her heart, hot flushes in her cheeks, dim mists before her eyes when she had thought about young Vanderlyn, of which she was suspicious—very. No; she was by no means sure that she knew nothing about love—but she did not say this to her father. Instead she pressed her dark head closer to his thick white mane.

"Love!" said she. "It is such a pretty word. Tell me something of it, father."

He smiled down at her. "Ah, you have some interest! Well, I tell you." Into his old eyes there came the deep and happy glow of reminiscence of bright days. She knew the look— always was it in them when he was thinking of her mother and never was it in them at any other time.

"Love," said he, "it is life's spring-time. Ah, your mother, Anna! Your dear mother! It is the splendor and the glory of the dawn." The old man's head was back, his eyes were closed and on his face there was a singularly sweet and simple smile, more like that of a youth than that of one whose years stretch far behind him. "It is the light that falls from heaven and turns this grim old world into a paradise. It is the hand of fate that grips the heart till we must follow— follow. We cannot hold back, my Anna; I could not hold back, your lovely mother, she could not hold back. Ah, one must follow when Love's hand is clasped about one's heart and leads! Some day you will understand and many things will then be clear to you. It is the glow of ardor in the eyes, reflected from the flame which burns deep in the heart—the flame which melts, which welds a link, a mystic bond, to bind for all eternity." He opened his eyes, now, and smiled at her. "That, liebschen—that is love—ah, that is love. Your mother taught me all about it. Be careful—careful, Anna—about love!"

"It sounds so splendid as you speak of it! How shall I know when it has come to me?"

The old man's caution was all gone; his fears now all forgotten. He was thinking of past days, dear days, young days.

"How shall you know?" he asked, and smiled again, this time in soft, affectionate derision. "You will not mistake. Mistake? It is impossible. When your heart leaps at the sound of his dear footsteps; when the world is empty till he comes and then is, ah, so full that you are crowded out of it into the valleys of a paradise; when little chills run over you one moment and the next the hot blood makes your cheeks into twin roses! How shall you know? Ah, there are many signs!"

"And do you think that such a love will ever come to me?"

"To you? Of course." The old man caught himself up short, just there, and lost his rapt expression. There were still hopes in his heart of realization for his daughter of all the brilliant dreams of his own youth—those dreams which had so sadly gone quite wrong. She must do nothing which would shut her from it if ever it should become possible. "Yes; it will come to you, of course; but not for a long time, and you must be very careful," he added in a greatly altered, less magnetic voice. "You must love no one until I tell you."

"Can one make love wait?"

"Ah—well—yes—one *must!*"

"But father—"

"Wait! You must not question me, mine liebschen; but, someday it may be that I shall no longer flute-play in a garden. Someday, maybe, things are better with us. You must wait a while, to see if that comes true. Then—then, when it *is* true, I pick out for you, ach! the handsomest, the bravest gentleman that I can find. I bring him to you, and I say: 'Anna, you love him!' That is all."

She was dismayed. This was not to her taste at all! "But father—"

The old German in his worry lest the life that she must lead as the companion to the rich New Yorker might induce her to let down the barriers of the exclusiveness which that which he could not, at present name, implanted in his very soul, looked sternly at her. He wished, now, to end the talk of it. "That, Anna," he said gravely, "that is all."

"But you tell me you will pick him out and bring him to me! Must he not love me?"

This again made him forget a little. It brought back other vivid memories of those bygone days when, young and ardent, he had gone to this girl's mother with his heart aflame.

"Love you? Yah; of course he loves you. You think love is a game of solitaire? But—he *will* love you, liebschen. To fall very much in love with you he has only once to see you. But, Anna, it is not with women as it is with men. *You* must *conceal* your love, until he speaks."

She smiled. "And, father, what shall I do then?"

"Do when he speaks? When comes the right man and tells you that he loves you, asking you to be his wife, mine Anna, you must answer: 'For this so great honor, sir, I thank you, and I give you in return my heart and hand.'"

Ah, the visions in his mind as he said this, of the far-off German village, of the dainty maiden standing there before a gallant youthful gentleman, trying to be as formal, when she placed her hand in his, as lifelong training in the stiff formalities of life had made him, in his embarrassment, while he told his great devotion to her! Thinking back along the path of years that led to that bright garden, how Herr Kreutzer smiled!

"How beautiful that sounds!" said Anna, softly. "'For this so great honor, I thank you, and I give you in return my heart and hand.'"

It brought the old flute-player back from the far garden.

"Do not practice on it yet," he said, without unkindness, but with a firm tone which gave his words almost the stern significance of a real order. "There is no hurry, liebschen, but, when the time is ripe for it, ah, it will come. Yah; it will come."

Her thoughts were full of all this talk of love and marriage as she went to Mrs. Vanderlyn's next morning, to take up again her routine of companion and instructor to the lady in the German language. She was not so very fond of Mrs. Vanderlyn. That lady was too much absorbed in her ambition to gain real importance in the social world to leave much time for being lovable to anybody but her son. That she was fond of him no one could doubt, but he was winning his own way, and did not need her mother care. It left her free for other things; it made the other things essential to her happiness. How empty is a mother's life when from it, out into the world, her only son goes venturing, none but a mother knows. Mrs. Vanderlyn had striven to fill hers with social episodes and had not done so to her satisfaction. There were things, she had discovered, which money, by itself, cannot accomplish and the learning had astonished her. She had thought a golden key would certainly unlock all gates. It had come to her as inspiration that the easy way for an American to gain social favor in New York, where, hitherto, gates have been closed to her, might be to purchase social favor, first, in England or in Germany and then come back with the distinction of it clinging like a perfume to her garments. But the purchase had not been an easy matter. Abroad, to her amazement, money had its mighty value, but only as a superstructure. There must be firmer stuff for the foundation—family. Her family was traced too easily—for the tracing was too brief. It ended with abruptness which was startling, two generations back, in a far western mining camp. Beyond that all the cutest experts in false genealogies had failed to carry it convincingly.

"Anna," she said to the attentive girl, "tell me about your family in Germany."

"My family?" said Anna. "There is no family of mine, now, left in Germany. My father—he is here with me, my mother died when I was very young. I can remember her a little, but *so* little that it makes my heart ache, for it is so ver-ry little."

"I mean about your grandfather and grandmother. Who were they and what were they? You are certainly well educated."

"My father and an old woman whom he hired, in London, have taught me what they could. I studied hard because I had so little else to do. It helped me in my loneliness. Ah, I was ver-ry lonely, ach! in London!"

"Had you no friends?"

"I had my father and my M'riarrr."

"Did no one ever visit you from Germany?"

"No one ever visited from anywhere."

"What did your father do, there?"

"He played first-flute in an orchestra—a theatre."

"Did he never go back to his home—his native land—to Germany, you know, to see his relatives?"

"I think he has no relatives alive."

"Did you never ask him about that?"

"If he had wish to tell me—if there had been some for to tell about—he would have told me without asking. I never thought of asking questions about such a thing."

"It's very funny!" Mrs. Vanderlyn said somewhat pettishly. "I could have sworn, from the first time I saw your father on the steamer, that he was a man of family."

"Of family? No; Mrs. Vanderlyn, I think not so."

"And he has never told you anything?"

"He has told me, sometimes, that by and by, when something happens which he never will explain, we would go back to Germany."

The daily lesson in court German then went on. Mrs. Vanderlyn was plainly disappointed at the meagreness of Anna's family history, and did badly with her lesson; but she could not possibly complain. Anna had made no claims. She had accepted her purely of her own—she did not realize how much it, really, had been her son's—volition. Anna had not asked for the position.

"I wonder," she was thinking, when she should have been absorbed in conjugations, "if there can be the slightest danger in my having this girl here. She's pretty and she has most charming manners. That accent is too fascinating, too. John might—but then, he is a boy of too much sense. If she only had been what I hoped she was, when I saw them on the steamer—but a mere flute-player's daughter! He would never be so silly."

On later days the lessons sometimes went with better speed and more enthusiasm; but almost always Mrs. Vanderlyn was occupied with thinking of the social life she knew and wished to know, so rapid progress was not possible.

John was out of town much of the time and when he came it was impossible for him to see much of the little German maiden, and this made Anna most unhappy. Deep in her heart she knew that what her father had described had come to her—she knew she loved; but it was all a mighty puzzle. Even if he loved her in return, of which she was by no means certain, he was not at all the sort of man, she thought, of whom her father would approve. Her father's notions were the notions of the stiff old world. He had said that she must wait until he was a flute-player no longer and that when that glad time came, he would, himself, pick out for her the handsomest and bravest gentleman whom he could find and bring him to her, ready-made, to love. She knew he felt a great contempt for riches; she knew that his experience of America had far from prepossessed him in favor either of the country or the people in it. She was absolutely certain that the man whom he would choose for her would be a very different sort of person from John Vanderlyn. Handsome he was, for certain, strong he was, for sure; but he was not a German and she knew that when her father spoke of "gentlemen" he had in mind none but a well-bred, well-born German.

It seemed to her, as she reflected on this matter, that she could not possibly endure to wed a German. She was, indeed, a little frightened by what her father had declaimed about her future and the matter of her courtship.

Then things happened, all at once, so suddenly that she could scarcely credit her own knowledge of them. One morning, coming in with Mrs. Vanderlyn from a long ride, she was informed that Herr Kreutzer had just been there with M'riar, and had left a note for her upon her dressing-table after having waited for a time. The note said that he had an unexpected holiday and begged her to come home, if possible, to spend it with him, and she was just coming out of Mrs. Vanderlyn's boudoir, where she had gone to get permission, when she unexpectedly met John. He had come home without notice and ahead of time from one of his long journeys.

CHAPTER VI

"Has she not come then, yet, my child?" said Kreutzer to the busy M'riar, as he returned. He had thought that Anna might have reached the tenement by that time, for he had gone out a second time and made a number of delightful, although meagre purchases.

"No signs," said M'riar. "Yn't see a sign of 'er. But hit cawn't be long before she'll be 'ere, can it?"

"No, M'riar; not long."

The place was poorly furnished. Marks of poverty, indeed, were everywhere; but upon the little table with its oil-cloth cover, soon began to show, as he brought package after package from his pockets, an array of goodies which amazed M'riar greatly. From the little gas-pipe chandelier which hung above the table (fly-specked and badly rusted before M'riar's busy hands had done their best to polish it, and still uncouth in its plain iron and sharp angles), he hung a little wreath of evergreen. Out of a package, with the utmost care, he produced a frosted cake.

"See, M'riar!" he cried.

"Hi sye!" said M'riar, examining it with distant care as if she

Edward Marshall and Charles T. Dazey

feared that it would either break or bite. "Won't she be took haback?"

"And," said Herr Kreutzer, delving busily in a pocket of his long, limp, overcoat, "a bottle of good wine."

"My heye!" said M'riar, awed and gaping admiration. "She *will* be took haback!"

"And, see again?" said Kreutzer, taking other treasures out of packages and pockets, including a roast fowl, and celery and other fixings. "It is not often, lately, that I have my Anna with me. When she comes, then we must do what we can do to make her welcome." He might have added that it was not often that a little stroke of luck brought him in money for a celebration such as this, but did not.

"*Such* a feast!" said M'riar.

"Ah, it is something," said the flute-player. "It is little I can do. I earn so little in this country—less, even, than I earned in London; and here all things cost so much—*more*, even, than they cost in London."

M'riar went to the window, after having seen the good things, while his hands went to his pocket and brought from it the door-key and a pocket-knife. He laughed a little bitterly. "The little feast has cost the last cent in my pocket! When night comes I must walk back to the Garden!... Well what matter? Anna is not suffering, and to-day she will be happy here with me."

"Hi, she's comin'," M'riar screamed and dashed out of the room.

Herr Kreutzer gazed after her with a wide smile of toleration.

She had not been a nuisance; she had been very useful. "I worried when we found her on the ship," said he, "and here she is, my housekeeper, while Anna is more happy in the mansion of the Vanderlyns! So things occur as we do not expect."

There came to him the sound of chattering voices on the stair. He hurried to the door.

"Anna, Anna!" he called into the hallway.

An instant later and she sprang up the last flight and ran into his opened arms. "Father!" she cried happily. There was an unwonted flush upon her cheeks, a new, soft glow within her eyes, a certain subtle dignity about her bearing which he failed to note, but which she knew was there and which the keener eyes of M'riar saw and were much puzzled by.

"Father!" she cried again, and held him in so close a clasp that his face reddened quite as much because she choked him as because his heart was beating high with happiness at sight of her.

"Come, come," said he, and led her to a chair by the window which commanded a small vista of back-yards—the only glimpse of out-of-doors the tiny tenement apartment offered. "My liebling! My little Anna! It is good to hold you so, again!" He clasped her in his arms.

"'Yn't it beautiful!" M'riar muttered, gazing at them. "W'ite as snow 'is 'air looks, w'en 'ers that is that dark, is hup hagainst it close, like that!"

"Dear old father!" Anna cried, as she drew back. She took him by the shoulders, now, and, with her beautifully modelled, firm young arms, held him away from her so that she might examine him. With loving scrutiny she studied every line of the old face. Instantly she noted the weary droop of tired eyelids. "Are you sure you are quite well?"

He smiled. "Always I am well, when you are with me. Always well when you are with me, Anna."

"You look tired. Ah, it is not easy for you when you play—"

His heart stood still for half-a-dozen beats. Could it be possible that she had learned how he had lied to her about the place in which he played? Had she learned that it was not a park of elegant importance?

"It is a fine, a splendid park," he interrupted. "Some day I shall take you there, with M'riar, and shall show you. Not at once. At present I must be quite sure to please and so must play without distraction. Your presence might confuse me, so that I could not give satisfaction; but, someday, when things are a little better—then I take you with me."

As he lied away her fears his soul was bitterly inquiring what his daughter who had such respect for him and for his music, would think if she could hear him as he stood upon a rough-board platform, or sat beside a cheap piano, pounded by a colored youth who kept a glass of beer on one end and a cigarette upon the other as he played. What would Anna think of her old father if she heard him tootle on his flute, with all the breath which he could muster, the strains of "Hot Time," an old favorite, or "Waltz Me Around Again, Willie," not quite so old, but infinitely more offensive than the frank racket of the negro melody to his sensitive ear? How would her artistic soul revolt if she should hear his flute—his precious flute!—inquiring if anybody there had seen an Irishman named Kelly?

"What do they like best, my father?" Anna asked him, still looking searchingly into his face, as if she saw signs there which did not reassure her. "Mozart, possibly, or Grieg?"

"I think it is 'An Invitation to the Dance,'" said he, and smiled again, more sweetly, more convincingly than ever. "'Around, around, around!'" he muttered, bitterly, sarcastically, as he turned away from her.

"What, father?"

"That melody, so sweet; those words, so full of lovely sentiment—they cling in my old mind, my liebschen," said Herr Kreutzer, to cover up his error. "They what you call it? Keep running in my head—ah, around, around within my head, my liebschen."

"Somehow, I am af-raid that you do not, really, like the place where you are playing."

"It is a fine, a splendid park, my Anna," Kreutzer cried in haste. "I am a grumbler—an old grumbler. My only real cause for complaint is that I must play so very loud for some" (his heart was sore with a humiliation of the night before), "while, for others, it is necessary that I plays so s-o-f-t-l-y—lest my flute disturb their conversation. I am puzzled, Anna, that is all. Quite all. There is no cause for you to worry." He placed his hand upon her shoulder, and, as he sank wearily to the stiff, wooden chair which was as easy as the room could boast, she dropped to her knees beside him.

Her heart was very full. Vividly she longed to tell him that the love, of which he had discoursed to her, had not come in the least as he had said it would—summoned by his counsel after he had searched and found the man whom he decided would be best for her to marry. No; love had not approached her logically, rationally, as result of careful thought by a third party; it had come, instead, as might a burglar, breaking in; an enemy, making an assault upon an unsuspecting city in the night. She had yielded up the treasures of the casket of her heart without a murmur to the burglar; the city had capitulated without fighting, without even protest. She was sure he would not find it easy to approve of her selection.

So she was not ready, yet, to tell him; she was not ready to destroy the happiness of this, their day together, as she feared that such a revelation must, inevitably.

"Hard times, father!" she said, temporizing. "But perhaps, sometime, they shall be changed. Perhaps *I* shall be rich, some day."

"Ah, Anna, no; such thoughts are what they call, up at the park, the—the—what is it? Ah, I have it—dream of the pipe. Rich we shall never be, my Anna."

"But it's *so* hard as it is. Only once-a-while can we be here together."

"Hard?" said he, and smoothed her hair. "You must not say that. It is so sweet when once-a-while it comes! It makes me so happy—"

"Dear!"

Depression seized him, now. Fiercely the thought rose in his mind that while he waited for these meetings with the keenest thoughts of joy, she, on the other hand, must look forward to them with emotions much less purely happy. That she was glad to be with him he did not doubt; he could not doubt; but what a contrast must his poor rooms offer to the luxurious surroundings of her other days! It would be only human if she yielded to an impulse to be critical, only human if, against her will, she felt contempt for his dire poverty. The black thought filled his soul with bitterness.

"Look," he said, and rose with a sudden gesture almost of despair. "What must you think of me, my liebschen? Poor little rooms! They are no place for you. Ah, no; for you the grand and beautiful home of Mrs. Vanderlyn!"

His scorn of self was written, now, so plainly on his face, in such fierce lines of deep contempt and loathing, that, as she looked at him, it frightened her. She, also, rose and lightly clasped her arms about his neck in an appeal.

"There, all the week," he went on with less virulence, "you have, as her companion, the happy life I wish for you, Ah, your old father does not grudge you that, my liebschen! And, after all, you do not falter in your love. My poverty does not make you forget me—eh?"

"Forget you, father? These hours are pleasantest of all! These hours with you here in these rooms which you say are 'poor' are far, far pleasanter to me than any hours at Mrs. Vanderlyn's."

"Ah, so," said he. "Yes, you come back to me and we are happy—very happy. It is my good luck—much better than I really deserve. Come, now, come. A little cake, a little wine, in honor of your visit. M'riar, M'riar—where have you gone, M'riar?"

From the other room the slavey came with reddened eyes.

"'Ere, sir; 'ere Miss." She was snuffling.

"Why, M'riar," said Kreutzer, in dismay! "What is it? Why

weep you?"

"Ho, it allus mykes me snivel w'en I sees you two together, that w'y. Hi cawn't *stand* it. 'Ow you love! It mykes me *'ungry*. Yuss, fair 'ungry. Nobody ain't hever loved *me* none—it mykes me 'ungry."

Quick with remorse and sympathy Anna pounced upon her and enfolded her in a great hug, realizing, for the first time, that, on entering, she had been too anxious to show her affection for her father, too full of worry over what she had, that day, to tell him, to remember M'riar.

"*Dear* M'riarrr!" she said softly. "Dear M'riarrr! We love you. Don't we father—love her?"

"Yah; sure we love her," Kreutzer answered heartily and patted the child's head. "We love her much."

"My heye!" said M'riar, happily, her sorrows quickly vanishing. "'Ow much nicer New York his than Lunnon!"

It was with the grace of an old cavalier that Kreutzer led his daughter to the table, and called her attention to the little feast he had prepared.

The small display of goodies would have seemed poor enough had she compared it to the everyday "light luncheons" at the Vanderlyns', but she did not so compare it. Back to the old days of modest plenty which they had known in London, to the days of almost actual need which they had known in New York City, went her mind, for its comparison, and thus she found the feast magnificent. With real fervor she exclaimed above it. Her pleasure was so genuine that the old flute-player was delighted. "How splendid!" she cried honestly.

Having placed her in her chair he began, at once, in the confusion of his joy, to cut the cake, ignoring, utterly, the chicken. She did not call attention to his absent-mindedness.

"It looks almost like a wedding cake!" said she and laughed —but then, suddenly, there flooded back on her remembrance of the secret she must tell him before she left the tenement that afternoon. It sobered her. How would he take the news that she had not been content to wait for him to bring to her his wonderful "brave gentleman?"

"Ah, you are thinking about weddings!" he said genially, still cutting at the cake. For an instant she imagined that she had aroused suspicions, but, quickly, she saw plainly that he was but lightly jesting. "Have a care, my Anna! Have a care!"

Suddenly her heart was filled with resolution. When would there be a better time than now in which to tell him her sweet secret? It could not be that he would be so very angry. His love for her, his longing that she might be happy, were, she knew, too great for that. And, later, when he knew Jack Vanderlyn as well as she had come to know him, he would realize, as she did, that nowhere in the world, not in the castles of the barons on the Rhine, not in the palaces of kings, could he or anyone find more genuine gentility than in this free-born unpretending young American.

"Father!" she said timidly.

"My girl," said he, without the least suspicion that her heart could, really, be touched by anyone in this cold land of crude democracy, "you must always come and tell me if your heart begins to flutter like a little bird. You—"

"Of—course, my father."

The matter had not in the least impressed him. As she turned and re-turned something in her hand beneath the table, and tried to rouse her courage to the point of making full confession, the old man quietly dismissed the subject.

"Now, a health to you, my Anna," he said gaily and raised high his glassful of cheap wine. "May the good God give you all the happiness your father wishes for you! More than that I cannot say, for I wish you all the happiness in all the world. Ah, when I look at you I am so full of joy! It is as if sweet birds were singing in my heart. Wait—you shall hear!"

Forgetting the great feast, as, seized by the impulse to express himself in the completest way he knew he turned from her with a bright smile, he crossed the tiny room and took down from the mantlepiece his flute.

"Ah, play for me!" she cried, delighted, both at the prospect of the music, which she loved with a real passion, and at the prospect of the brief reprieve the diversion would afford her from the revelation which she had to make.

He pretended shy reluctance. "No; in your heart you do not really wish to hear. You have grown tired of the old flute, long ago."

She laughed and rose and went to him. "Bad boy! He must be teased! I am *not* tired of it. To me it is in all the world, the sweetest music. Must I say more? Come, come, for me!"

"Ah, then—for you!"

He raised the old flute to his lips and settled it beneath the thatch of whitened hair which covered his large, sensitive mouth. He took a little breath of preparation. Then he closed his eyes and played.

Such music as came from that flute! It was as if the "sweet birds singing in his heart" had risen and were perched, all twittering and cooing, chirping, carolling upon his lips. And all they sang about was love—love—love—a father's love for his delightful daughter. Sweet and pure and wholly lovely was the melody which filled the room and held the charming woman it was meant for spellbound; held the little slavey from the grime of London as one hypnotized upon her chair; sang its way out of the window, down into the grimy court between this dingy tenement and the whole row of dingy tenements which faced the other street, and made a dozen little slum-bred children pause there in their play, in wonder and delight. Ah, how Kreutzer played the flute, that day, for his beloved Anna!

"Ah, when you play," said she, as with a smile, he laid the wonderful old instrument upon the shelf again, "it is your life, your soul—you put all into the old flute!"

"Yes, Anna; and to-day it was far more. It was my love for you—that was the greatest part of it; and there were sweet memories of my native land." The fervor of his playing, more than the effort of it, had exhausted him. He sat down somewhat wearily, with a long sigh. "But we will not speak of our native land, my Anna," he said sadly. "Ach! I am a little tired." He held his arms out to her. "But happy—very happy," he said quickly when he saw the look of quick compassion on her face. "And you?"

The burden of her secret had grown heavy on her heart. It did not seem a decent thing to wait a moment more before she told it to him.

"I am happy, too—but—but—oh, my father, father!"

She threw herself into his arms, bursting into tears.

CHAPTER VII

The old flute-player looked down upon his lovely daughter as, sobbing, she clung to him, with bewildered, utterly dismayed amazement. What could be the matter with the child? He glanced about him helplessly. It dazed him. Everything, a moment since, had been so bright and gay! There had been a smile upon her lips, a soft glow of happiness alight within her eyes. He could not understand this situation. He was actually frightened.

So, also, was M'riar, who stood gaping at the spectacle of her Miss Anna's grief with wide, fear-stricken eyes.

"Cawn't Hi do nothink for 'er, sir?" she said, approaching timidly.

For the first time in his life he spoke almost harshly to the child, in his excitement. "No," he said emphatically. "You will only stand and say 'My heye! Hi sye! Hi sye! My heye!' You can do nothing. It would be well for you to step into the kitchen, possibly. I smell me that there may be something burning, there. And do not come again until I call to you. If nothing burns there, now, then something might burn, later. It would be well for you to stay and watch." He had no wish to hurt the poor child's feelings—but his Anna! Surely none but he must witness this completely inexplicable, this mad outburst of wild woe.

"What is this, my Anna?" he said softly to the weeping girl who clung there in his arms when M'riar had left the room. "You are tear-ing, Anna—you are tear-ing, child!" He was sure his English had escaped him, but he could not stop to make correction.

She looked up at him, at last. "'Tear-ing? Tear-ing?' Oh, crying! Yes, I'm crying—because I am so happy, and because—"

He was more puzzled by this extraordinary statement than he had been by her tears. "Because you are so *happy*! Hein! A woman—she is strange. So strange. She cries because she is so happy, then she cries because she is so sorry. When she cries no one can tell which makes her do it. You are sure it is the happiness, this time, that makes you cry?"

"Quite sure," said Anna, trying hard to stifle the great sobs. "Yes; I am certain. It is because I am so happy, and— because—I am a little bit—af-fraid!"

"You are afraid, my child? What is it fears you?"

She slipped out of his arms. There was no going back, she now must tell him all. She knew that he would not be harshly angry, though she greatly feared he would be sorely grieved.

She held him, with a gentle hand, back in his chair as he would have arisen, and sank down at his feet, her arm upon his knee, her face upturned. "Come, father," she said simply. "I want to sit here at your feet. I want to sit here at your feet just as I did when I was, oh, a very little girl!"

The old man was sorely puzzled, but he sank back in his

chair and let her take his hands—both of them. One of them she placed upon her beautiful, dark hair; the other she held close clasped against her bosom in her own. "Father, I have something to confess."

He was amazed, but less distressed than he had been. His Anna, his own, liebling Anna, could not have anything to confess which was so very terrible. He looked down at her and smiled in reassurance. Her wonderful, dark eyes were upturned, as he gazed, and, for an instant, looked straight at his; but then the delicately veined lids drooped.

"You have something to confess? What is it, Anna?"

"I shall not go back again to Mrs. Vanderlyn's," she slowly answered. "I have come home, my father; have come home to you—to stay."

He was worried. Could she be satisfied, after what she had been having there at Mrs. Vanderlyn's, with what his small purse had to offer her in this unpleasant tenement? His heart leaped at the thought of having her with him again; none but himself could know how greatly he had missed her, and he could give her food and shelter. But would she, now, be happy there with him, in all his poverty?

"Ah; you have quarreled?" he ventured, hesitantly.

"No," she faltered.

His wrath rose. Ah, that was it! The woman had been unkind to her, had asked of her some menial service, had presumed upon the fact that she was but an employee! "She has mistreated you," he cried, in indignation. "She has mistreated you! Well, here is—"

Anna interrupted him by laying a soft hand upon his lips. She had to stretch and strain a little to reach up so far, crouched low there, as she was, quite at his feet. Her heart was beating very fast as came the time for her confession. She hoped that he would not be very angry, very greatly horrified.

"No," she said slowly; "no, we have not quarreled, she has not mistreated me; but—she will be very angry—she will not forgive me, when she knows—"

Kreutzer was affrighted. There seemed to him to be a hint of dreadful revelations to be made in the soft droop of Anna's head, the trembling of her little hand in his, the swift ebb and flow of the rich color in the pink satin of her cheeks.

"Anna," he said, aghast, "what is there for her to know? Oh, my Anna—what is there for her to know? Fear not. Your old father—he will understand and will forgive—will forgive anything in all this world—no matter what. Remember that. Remember that, and tell me, Anna, what is there for Mrs. Vanderlyn to pardon?"

She did not lift her head. Her eyes flashed up at him in one quick look of terror, but never by an inch did she raise toward her father's, now, her pale, affrighted face. "It was a great temptation, father," she said slowly. "A very great temptation."

Now he was alarmed, indeed. "Anna," he demanded, in a voice that was not like his own, "what have you done? What have you done?"

Every horrid thought—but one—which could flash into being in the human mind at such a time, rushed into his, in a terrific jumble of mad speculations.

For a moment Anna cowered, alarmed by what a quick glimpse of his face had shown her. She had never seen a human face so—not whitened by his fear, but greyed—greyed as if seared with fire and turned to carven ashes. She could tell, by that, that he would never, really, forgive her. Too firmly had his hopes been fixed upon the plans which he had built in many long hours of reflections going back along the years, no doubt, to that far time when she was lying, a mere babe, in her dear mother's arms. How ardently she wished, now, at this crisis, that that mother might be there to soften things for her; to turn his wrath, explain, make clear to him the fact that there are impulses too strong for women's hearts to put aside!

She did not look at him again—she could not bear to see that face again—but slowly rose and slowly crossed the little room to the crude table and took from it her handbag, which, when M'riar had cleared off the dinner things, she had replaced where it had been when she had started, first, to lay the table. As she raised the bag her father's eyes were fixed upon her in an agony of dread.

Trembling with apprehension, her fingers shaking so that it was with great difficulty that she managed the bag's clasp, she opened the receptacle, and, with accelerating nervousness which made her feel and fumble, took from it a small box—a jeweler's box. Slowly she returned to him, her feet dragging as if weighted; slowly, as she stood before him, drooping, frightened, she took off the cover of the little box, her heart hammering till it seemed as if it must burst from her breast; slowly, then, with trembling fingers, while her eyes remained steadfastly downcast and the quick rising, falling, of her delicately rounded, girlish bosom showed how keen her agitation was, she took from the opened box a sparkling trinket.

"You will understand me, father, when I show you—"

She held the brilliant bauble towards him, and, as she stretched out her hand a hundred little facets on the glittering thing caught light, there in the gloomy tenement house room, and blazed and sparkled as with inner fires.

"Look, father."

The old flute-player stretched a wondering hand to take the trinket. He could not understand, at all, what all this meant. What had the thing to do with her great agitation? How came she with so valuable a jewel? What did it mean—all of it? What under heaven could it mean?

"A ring? Ah," said he, "it is a beautiful ring set with a diamond. Where did you get it, Anna?" He laid it upon the table quickly. He did not seem to wish to hold it in his hand.

This was the crucial moment and she looked at him with dumb appeal in her fine eyes. Then, seeing nothing in his face to reassure her, she dropped her gaze. Her chest heaved with a quick sob.

"My dear, my dear," she now began, "I have a great confession. Do not, please, be angry with me, father! I must tell you—"

She was interrupted by a quick, sharp rap upon the door. There was in it the abrupt demand of an official visitation, and it startled both of them.

Hastily she rose and stood gazing at the closed door; wonderingly he rose, also, and, poised, ready to go and open it, waiting a second, to see if there would be a repetition of the knock.

"Who is there?" he called, at length.

"I, Mrs. Vanderlyn," came the reply, in high-pitched, angry tones.

"M'riar," the flute-player called loudly, "go to the door."

Anna, now very plainly much alarmed, cowered back against the table, her face turned toward the door, her two hands back of her, caught desperately on the table and supporting her. Kreutzer looked at her with new alarm—a dreadful apprehension. What could the girl have done to be thus frightened by the coming of the woman whose employment she had left?

"Mrs. Vanderlyn!" the girl gasped, weakly.

Then Kreutzer saw her do a thing which added to his great amazement, his great worry. With a quick stride she crossed the little space between her and the table, quickly snatched from it the box and ring, put the cover on the box, and, hurriedly, with almost furtive gesture, thrust the box into her handbag, being careful, he observed, to see to it that in the bag it was well covered by a handkerchief and veil.

"Why do you look so frightened?" he demanded, in a voice now hoarse and painful.

Anna was as pale as death as she replied: "I am afraid she has discovered—"

"Discovered?" said her father, a grim light breaking on his confused faculties. Ah, this was terrible, but must be faced! Ah, God! His little Anna! She had taken it—had stolen it— from Mrs. Vanderlyn! But he would stand by her. Nothing should induce him to abandon her, no matter what mad thing she had been tempted into doing. Doubtless it had been his poverty (and was his poverty not direct result of his incompetence?) which had led her into doing the dread thing which he began to understand that she had done.

Now, surely, was not the time for him to offer her reproaches. Now was the time, when he, the best friend she had, could ever have, must comfort her and shelter her. Later, if there were reproaches to be offered, would be time enough to offer them.

"Hush!" he said cautiously. "How you tremble! Anna—my little Anna! She shall not see you like this. Go, liebling. I will first speak to her. And ... whatever it may be ... fear not. Fear not."

M'riar had come in, and, fascinated by the scene, began to dimly see its awful import, also. Her training in the slums of London where a knock like that upon the door meant but one thing—the law—made the situation clear to her, at once, and, bewildered as she was by the amazing fact that it was Anna—her Frow-line—who was involved, she did not lose her head.

"This w'y," she whispered, hoarsely. "This w'y, Frow-line! This w'y!"

She hurried Anna out into the kitchen and the flute-player could hear the key turn in the lock behind them. Sure that, for the moment, his dear child was safe, he now went to the door, with measured, steady tread, and opened it.

"Come, Madame, come," he said to Mrs. Vanderlyn, who, flushed and angry, waited with small patience at the threshold.

The old flute-player caught the glint of polished buttons and a polished shield upon the breast of a man's coat beyond her, and he recognized the face above them as that of his old shipboard enemy, Moresco, now policeman on this beat.

CHAPTER VIII

The superbly dressed visitor, wrapped in silk brocades and woven feathers, seemed strangely out of place there in the doorway of the dingy tenement apartment. That she felt herself so, also, was apparent, for there was, upon her face, a look of high contempt and keen distaste. She swept into the little room with all the majesty of a proud queen, forced, by some untoward circumstance, to call at the low hovel of a very, very humble, and, probably, unworthy subject.

"Ah, Herr Kreutzer."

The old flute-player, after a scared glance into the hallway, where he had thought he saw the flash of brazen buttons, bowed low and handsomely. Among all the millionaire male friends of Mrs. Vanderlyn was not one who was half capable of such a bow, and, in a dim way she appreciated this. She did not for a moment, though, think it marked the aged man before her as a gentleman, and worthy, therefore, of consideration from a lady. She was trying to feel certain, now, that what she had believed an evidence of really high breeding, was, really, mere clever sham. The old musician had lost all the glamor of his mystery for her. Surely, had he really been what she suspected, then his daughter would have been incapable of the offense which she, its victim, had come there to punish. Now the old man's courtly grace upon the ship, by which she had been fooled into believing him a person of real eminence, was openly revealed to her as counterfeit and worthless—he was a swindler, almost, indeed, as viciously dishonest as the thing his daughter had been guilty of. Now his manner merely sent a vague reflection through her brain that upon the ocean's other side their peasants were well trained. Now she was bitterly resentful of the fact that, on the ship, she had been fooled into thinking him a person, possibly, of eminence.

"So," said Kreutzer, offering her, with graceful courtesy which made her falter in her new conviction, and a perfect ease, withal, which much astonished her, the best chair in the room. "And you, Madame, are Mrs. Vanderlyn?"

"Yes," Mrs. Vanderlyn replied. "I'm Mrs. Vanderlyn. Your daughter, till to-day, was—my companion."

"Ah, Madame; I know," said the old man. "You wish to see her? Is that the reason why you honor my so humble home, Madame?"

Mrs. Vanderlyn, who had come to bluster, was a bit non-plussed, even a bit abashed by the superb and easy manner of the man. Never in her life had she been privileged, indeed, to meet with a reception so graceful and so courteous. Could she, after all, be wrong? Here, at last, in an apartment on the top floor of a New York tenement, had she encountered what she had vainly searched for, elsewhere, even on her travels in the European countries. This was the grace and courtesy which she had read about. She really was much impressed, and, in her heart, would have been pleased if she had had an errand there less disagreeable. She wondered why she had not remembered with more accuracy, the superb demeanor of this aged man on shipboard. If she had only realized—she even might have dressed him up, she speculated, and had him at her house for dinner! She could have introduced him to her climbing friends as a musician of great eminence, abroad (she remembered with regret, now, that he really played the flute magnificently—so everyone on shipboard had exclaimed), and made them envious to a degree. But now that she had started on this task, she would not falter. She assured herself, indeed, that duty as a citizen demanded that she should *not* falter.

"Yes," she said to him, with real regret, "I certainly must see your daughter; but I am glad first to explain to you—"

"The pleasure," said the courtly flute-player, "is mutual, Madame. May I ask you what you must explain?"

Mrs. Vanderlyn now summoned to her face a look of sympathy, lugubrious and as sincere as she could make it. "It will be a blow, Herr Kreutzer."

The old man was uneasy, but he hid it as best he could, under a most careful, unremitting courtesy. "A blow, Madame?"

She did not speak, at once, but stood there looking at him with wide eyes which she was very careful to make sad. It made him madly nervous.

"Well, I am ready," he protested, after the delay became intolerable. "I beg of you do not delay."

"First," said Mrs. Vanderlyn, not going to the heart of the unhappy matter, as his whole soul begged of her to do, but paltering with an unnecessary explanation, "you must understand the arrangement of my house. My son's room adjoins my own; then comes the little boudoir I assigned to Anna; then—"

"Yes, Madame," said Kreutzer, unable to endure this any longer, "but what of that? You said—"

"I am positive that this afternoon no one was near those rooms but Anna."

Kreutzer was in agony. "Go on, Madame," he said, imploringly. "Do you not see that this is torture? I cannot bear it longer."

She looked at him again, with that assumed expression of compassion, and he could have torn her secret from her with hooked fingers, so exasperated, so intensely agonized was he by her delays. Finally he made a desperate, downward, begging gesture with both hands, and, understanding, she went on:

"This afternoon my son returned from somewhere, and went into his room. He did not come into my room to call me, as he sometimes does. He was very quiet and it made me curious. I thought perhaps the boy might be there suffering with some headache, or something, which he did not wish to bother me about. A mother's heart, you know—"

"Madame, I pray you, have some consideration for a father's heart, and hasten."

"I went into his room to speak to him and found that he had left it; but on his table was a little jewel-box."

The flute-player drew in his breath with a sharp hiss, so close set were his teeth. Now she was coming to it! Now she was coming to the accusation of his Anna—the accusation which —ah, God!—had been preceded by the girl's own terrible confession.

"Yes," said he, trying not to let his eyes turn toward the bag, which still lay on the table, "a jewel-box. Well, Madame, what of that?"

"Being a woman," Mrs. Vanderlyn said slowly, "I could not withstand the temptation. I looked in. Within I saw—a magnificent diamond ring."

Still she had not reached the crux of what she had to say. Would the woman never come to the great point—would she never make the charge against his Anna definite and clear? "Well?" he said unhappily, and, as he said the word a resolution found birth in his brain. His little Anna! What if she had been tempted and had yielded? He would not let her suffer for it, as this cold and haughty woman evidently wished to have her suffer! He would ward disgrace from her—at any cost.

Carefully, so that the movement could not rouse suspicion in the mind of his exasperating visitor, he put his hand behind him and let it fall on the bag upon the table. Once on it, his fingers worked with skill and that precision which is natural to fingers trained by practice on a musical instrument until they seem to have a real intelligence, scarcely dependent on the brain.

"I knew for whom the dear boy meant that jewel," Mrs. Vanderlyn went on. "He had bought it as a present for me on my birthday, which occurs tomorrow."

Kreutzer nodded slowly, his fingers working, all the time, in Anna's bag. "Presents are sometimes made on birthdays," he admitted. "Well?"

"Happy in the thought that he had remembered me, I went out for my drive, leaving the box there on his table, just where I had found it. When I reached the house again I found a note left for me by your daughter, saying that she had decided upon going from my house forever, that someday she hoped I would forgive her—"

"What had she done?" said Kreutzer, in a dry voice, full of misery.

"Ah, that she did not say." Mrs. Vanderlyn paused now, with a fine sense of the dramatic. "But immediately I looked again for that box and ring and they—were gone!"

Kreutzer, pale, his forehead damp from perspiration of pure agony, as truly sweat of pain as any ever beaded on the brow of an excruciated prisoner upon the rack, looked at her with pleading eyes. "Gone! Madame, you do not think—"

She smiled a bitter little smile. There was, also, just a touch of triumph in it, such as small souls show when they are on the point of proving to another, even though a stranger, that they have been wrong in trusting someone, believing in some thing. "My dear sir," she said slowly, not from unwillingness to speak but to give emphasis, "what else can I think? No one but my son, myself and Anna had been near that room—"

Kreutzer straightened up as one whose shoulders have been stooped for the reception of a mighty load which, finally, has been fixed upon them. "You have told him?"

"Not yet."

"Ah, that is lucky.... I beg your pardon, Madame, you have dropped your handkerchief."

The handkerchief had fallen not less than a minute before, and, instinctively, he had started forward, intending to restore it to her; but by that time the situation had begun to be quite clear to him—ah, deadly clear to him!—and, in a flash the strategy had come to him. Knowing, then, that that dropped handkerchief would be essential to its execution, he had let it lie.

Mrs. Vanderlyn turned carelessly to raise the handkerchief, and, as she turned, he carried out his plan. Quick as a flash, he slipped the box which held the ring, out of the bag and into his own pocket. When she straightened up again, after having (with a flush, for he had seemed exceedingly polite, before) recovered her own handkerchief, she found him standing as he had stood, only, possibly, a little more erect than he had been, with some addition of calm dignity to his carriage, with a calmer look in his old eyes.

"Why is it lucky that I have not told him?" Mrs. Vanderlyn asked, now. "Of course he'll have to know. Everyone must know."

It broke his self-control. "That—my little girl is—no, no, no!" he faltered. "Ah, it is not true! She is not guilty!"

She tried to show a sympathetic smile, but in it there was little actual sympathy. "Very natural that you should think so," she admitted. "It came as a great shock—and a surprise —even to me. I had thought she was unusually well-bred, refined." She sighed, as if the world were rather hard on her, to fool her so in one she had believed to be an admirable person. "But let me tell you that she has great admiration for fine jewels. I have noted that, before. And—the temptation was too strong for her. Weak spot, somewhere, in her, don't you see? It was too strong for that weak spot."

"Oh, Madame, I—"

She raised her hand as if to ward away his protests. Clearly she believed that having told him all about it, as gently as she had, she had accomplished her whole Christian duty and was under not the slightest further obligation to be merciful. "I may as well tell you," she warned him, "that I brought an officer with me. To save your natural feelings, I requested him to wait downstairs a moment and then to come and wait outside the door—er—um—in case of trouble. Just a little necessary precaution, my dear sir. A woman, coming to a place like this, alone, you see—"

He smiled. "Quite natural," he answered. "Why, I might have eaten you!" But in the absorption of his talk with her he had forgotten that, as he went to the door, he had seen a blue coat and brass buttons, had recognized the face of his old enemy, Moresco. Now the realization that, armed and uniformed, a minion of the forces of the city's law and order, that cheap foe was actually waiting for his little Anna—for his gentle, big-eyed, soft-voiced Anna!—came to him with a new and dreadful shock. His frame stiffened and his poor old, soft hands clenched into pathetic fists. "He shall not—" he began with a brave bluster, but then stopped, realizing his own helplessness.

"What can you do?" asked Mrs. Vanderlyn, and smiled again that twisted little smile which was her counterfeit of the sweet look of sympathy. "I am only doing what is right and what is necessary. I am, naturally, most indignant at this betrayal of my confidence. I will not interfere to save the girl from justice!"

From behind the kitchen door, at this, Herr Kreutzer thought he heard a sound as of swift breath indrawn through tight-set, angry teeth, but was not sure. It might have been his own. He was so terribly excited that he did not know. Certainly, from now, his angry breathing was quite audible. His little Anna taken to a prison! No! "She shall not be punished!" he exclaimed in wrath.

Mrs. Vanderlyn looked at him, for a second, as might one look at an unpleasant child who is a disappointment. Then she for the first time showed a little wrath towards him. Up to that moment her calm, maddening attitude of skin-deep sympathy had been unbroken. She spoke sharply, now, however, as she countered: "That will not depend on you."

"It *shall* depend on me!" said Kreutzer, hotly.

"There is but one thing which will lighten the severity of the bad girl's punishment," said Mrs. Vanderlyn, didactically.

"And that, Madame?"

"The immediate restitution of the ring. She is here, now, is she not?"

"Yes, she is here, but—"

The poor old man looked helplessly around him. The whole thing seemed too terrible to be believed. He wondered if some dreadful nightmare did not hold him prisoner and half expected, as he let his agonized old eyes roam round the room, to wake up, presently, and find the episode was but a dreadful dream.

"Call her; ask her to give it up—"

"No," said the old man softly, careful that his voice should not rise so that it could easily be audible in the adjoining room, "I will not ask her to give up the ring, for the ring is not in her possession. She would not know of what I spoke. She would look at me, my Anna would, with soft reproach in her sad eyes and wonder if her poor old father had gone mad to bring an accusation such as that against her soul—so pure—so innocent—so—"

"Certainly she has the ring." The woman, now, was definitely sneering at his protestations of his daughter's worthiness.

"No; she has not got the ring. I—have it—"

From his pocket he drew forth his hand and in it lay the little box. Out of the box, with trembling fingers, he removed the ring, and held it up, smiling at her, as he did so, with a wondrous look of triumph—not the look of one who has just placed his feet, quite consciously, upon the road that leads to prison, but that of one who has won victory against great odds. She could not understand that look.

And that was not so strange, for on the face of the old flute-player the expression was like few this selfish old world ever sees—the expression of complete self-abnegation, of absolute self-sacrifice for pure and holy love.

"The ring, Herr Kreutzer!" Mrs. Vanderlyn exclaimed, in relief, sure, now, for the first time, of the recovery of the precious trinket. "The ring! She's given it to you!"

Herr Kreutzer laid the box upon the table and drew back with studied calm to gaze at her reflectively, as is necessary to a man who, as he stands and talks, must fashion from his fancy a cute fiction logical enough and clear enough to save from overwhelming sorrow one whom he loves better than he loves himself. "I tell you the whole truth," he said, "on one condition. One condition, mind you, Madame—and that condition must be kept. It is that she—my Anna—shall never be disturbed, annoyed—"

The woman shook her head with emphasis. Self-righteous and indignant, feeling that her confidence had been betrayed as well as her ring stolen, she was determined not to let the guilty girl escape. "I cannot promise that," she said with emphasis, "for she is guilty."

The German raised himself to his full height and stood there towering over her, the very effigy of sublime fatherhood. "She is *not* guilty!" he exclaimed. "No; it is I—I—I!"

"You!" Mrs. Vanderlyn fell back a step or two, staring at him in amazement. Could the man be crazy? This unexpected turn of the affair brought a gasp of sheer astonishment from her.

From behind the door Herr Kreutzer thought he heard, again, a sound as of swift breath drawn through tight shut teeth, but again he was not sure—nor did it matter. When, an instant later, the door softly opened, then as softly closed and left M'riar there in the room with them, standing, for a second, with her back against the portal which she had just come through, neither of them glanced at her. The situation which involved them was too tense, too fiercely was their full attention focussed upon one another. They scarcely noted that she passed as she went through the room and out the other door.

"Yes," said Herr Kreutzer, "it is I who took the ring."

CHAPTER IX

"*You* who took the ring!" said the astonished woman. "How utterly absurd! You have not been in my house." She was so amazed by his confession, which, she knew, could not have the least foundation, that, for the moment, she forgot to pose, either as an injured benefactress or as an avenging nemesis.

Now Herr Kreutzer smiled. Having determined on the sacrifice, he was delighted by this first error in her argument. "Yes, Madame," he said, quite truthfully, "I *have* been at your house. I called while you were driving. M'riar will tell you. She went with me. I called there to tell Anna that I should expect her here, this afternoon. A servant showed me to her room—showed M'riar and me both to her room. I can prove all of this by M'riar—by your own servants, Madame. I waited for her, for a time, there in her room, and, as I walked to and fro, I saw, through an open door, upon a table—that jewel-box."

Mrs. Vanderlyn was looking at him in complete astonishment. Even in her artificial soul there rose some admiration for the man who would confess to felony, rather than submit his child to suffering.

"And you—," she cried.

He bowed before her, almost as he had, in bygone days, bowed low before an appreciative audience. Was not this, as much as ever any solo on the flute had been, a triumph of high art? And more! Was it not the triumph of his love for Anna over, first, this hard-souled, little-minded Mrs. Vanderlyn, and, second, the last selfish impulse lingering within his own unselfish soul?

"I am very, very poor, Madame," he said. "I am only a poor flute-player. Things have not gone well with me since I have been in your so great, so glorious country. No; they have gone very far from well with me. If they had not gone most ill do you imagine that I ever would have let my Anna go to you as your companion? Do you not imagine that it cut my soul to have her separate from me, that it cut my pride to have to tacitly admit that I was quite unable to provide for her? Yes, Madame; it cut both soul and pride. But I am very poor. What could I do? I am so poor that always I have little to wear—see, Madame, this old suit is all that I possess! It prevents me, possibly, from getting better wages than I might get if I were not so shabby. Often, also, I do not have enough to eat. That, Madame, is true, although my Anna does not know it. Well, glittering in that little box upon the dresser, when I was there at your house, I saw so much comfort, so much happiness."

The old man's art had won, indeed. He had quite convinced the woman that it had been he and not his daughter who had stolen the diamond.

She was not exactly disappointed, although it robbed the crime of one of its most dramatic elements—ingratitude. She was being quite as well diverted by the old man's dignity and calm as she would have been by his poor Anna's wild, hysterical grief. She was, perhaps, she thought, a very lucky woman. She had not only had a valuable diamond stolen, which, of itself, was entertaining, in a way, but she had recovered it through such a strange experience as would furnish food for tales to be told in boudoirs and over tea-cups for three months.

"So it really was you!"

"Yes, yes; have I not told you?"

There was an inconsistency in this affair, however, and Mrs. Vanderlyn thought herself a veritable Sherlock Holmes as she pounced on it. "But that note from Anna?" she protested.

Kreutzer had been thinking of that note from Anna, and, for a time, had found the obstacle a hard one to surmount. At length, and in good time to meet the question, he had, however, arranged an explanation, which, if not too carefully looked into, would seem reasonable.

"Oh, of course," said he. "You mean the note about her going away? Why, that is easily to be understood. When she came I told her that I have had luck. I told her that we have much money and we go to Germany, at once. I was afraid that if she went back to your house there would arise suspicions, so I said she must not go, but must be content with just the note, alone, for her goodbyes. She did not wish to do this, but consented, at the last, because I ordered her to do it."

Mrs. Vanderlyn was now entirely convinced. He had made the case against himself so black she could not doubt it; but she determined that if he thought he would gain clemency in payment for the frankness of his full confession he would find himself to be mistaken. It was her duty as a member of society, she told herself, to see to it that the guilty poor who prey upon the helpless rich should not pass on unpunished.

"I understand," she said, "you are the guilty one. Your daughter is quite innocent of this. It may be chance, alone, that keeps her so. With such a father—but I will be merciful and will not show you what a vile inheritance of wickedness you have prepared for the poor child. Your conscience will do that, if you have any conscience. While you are in prison you will have that to reflect upon."

He was dismayed. The ring had been returned. Would she still—"I—I must go to prison?"

"Why, certainly. Don't you see how necessary that is? What would happen to society if thieves were left unpunished?"

"Thief!" The word fell on his ears with tragic force. A thief in prison! Was this to be the end of all his striving? Were the high hopes and ambitions of his splendid youth to end, at length, behind the bars of a thief's cell? Ah, those happy, bygone days, when with unbounded hope and confidence he had promised all things to the lovely creature he had wooed and won and wed in that toy village far away in the Black Forest! What was their fruition! Unhappiness, disgrace and exile for her loveliness, and finally a child for whom she paid the supreme price of death. His promises, breathed at her bedside of unwavering care, unfaltering devotion, unfailing happiness for the wee baby in the years to come— how had he kept them? Poverty, distress, privation. With such commodities had he redeemed those promises, and, finally, had driven the girl, naturally as sweet-souled as an angel, as pure as the new-fallen snow, to vulgar crime to satisfy, no doubt, those girlish and quite natural desires which it should have been his duty and his pleasure to provide for. Oh, he had done well with life! The soul within him writhed in agony as he reflected on the use which he had made of it. His heart went sick from shame. And—what would Anna do without him?

"Ah, yes, Madame; I see," said he. "I see. Society must be protected from such folk as I. Yes; that is very clear indeed. We menace it. The place for us is where stone walls surround us—to protect society; locks hold us—to protect society; death comes quickly to us—to protect society. I see all that, Madame. I will go to prison as a punishment, of course. But you will let me see my Anna for a moment—you will let me say goodbye to Anna? She is here, in the next room. I had hoped, you see, that I could make you think that prison was not necessary; I had hoped that I could fool you into thinking that I was not, very much, a danger to society. But you have found me out. You realize how terrible I am. When I thought that I could fool you I had her go to the next room, so that, perhaps, she might know nothing of it. Now, of course, she will know all, but—you will let me say goodbye to her? You will wait for me, out here?"

Mrs. Vanderlyn was not too willing, but, as she thought of it, it seemed quite safe, and she could tell her friends, she rapidly reflected, that she had been swayed by irresistible impulse of mercy. That would sound well, told dramatically.

"I suppose so," she said grudgingly. "But any attempt at escape will be useless. You—"

He looked at her with a sad dignity.

"I shall not try to escape," he said. "I only ask that if it can be done, as long as it may be possible to do it, my Anna shall not know about my sin, discovery, disgrace. Let her think, please, Madame, if you will, that I have gone on a long journey."

This, too, she granted grudgingly. "Oh, very well, if you imagine such things *can* be hidden. I won't tell her. Just as you wish."

"You will wait here for me while I say goodbye to her?"

"Well, don't be long."

The old flute-player was turning towards the kitchen door, when a loud rap upon the hall door halted him.

"I suppose the officer has grown tired of waiting," Mrs. Vanderlyn explained.

"Come in," said Kreutzer, wonderingly. Few visitors had ever knocked at his door since he had moved to that tenement.

To Mrs. Vanderlyn's amazement, and his own, the door, when it had opened, revealed John Vanderlyn. He was very plainly worried. He did not even stop for greetings, but said, immediately, to his mother:

"Well, mother, what are you doing here?"

Mrs. Vanderlyn was quite as much surprised, apparently, to see him there, as he was to discover her in the old flute-player's rooms.

"My dear boy!" she cried. "How in the world did you learn that I had come here? What do you want? Has something happened at the house?"

Her son advanced into the room with a low bow to his host. It was quite plain that, for some reason, he wished to show Herr Kreutzer every courtesy; it was plain that he had reason to suspect that, possibly, his mother had not done so and that this fact worried him.

"The butler heard you give the order to the chauffeur to drive you to Herr Kreutzer's home," he told his mother briefly. Then, turning to Herr Kreutzer, he said earnestly: "My dear sir, if my mother has said anything harsh or disagreeable to you—"

Kreutzer was astonished, but had no complaint to make. His only wish was, now, to have his opportunity to bid his girl farewell and then to go to prison, where, as quickly as was possible, he might serve out whatever sentence was imposed on him. After his release, if the sentence was not of such duration that it spanned the few short years of life remaining to him, he would once again work for his Anna and endeavor to atone to her for the misfortunes which his own incompetence, he argued, had oppressed her with.

"Your mother," he assured the youth, so that the situation might not be prolonged, "has been polite. Your mother has been most polite."

The young man, with an expression of relief upon his face, turned then, to his mother. "Tell me, mother, what has brought you here," he said.

She did not hesitate. The situation did not in the least depress her. Rather was she somewhat proud of her own part in it. "It's really painful, my dear boy," said she, "but I flatter myself that I've been quite a Sherlock Holmes. I suppose you haven't even discovered, yet, that the diamond ring is gone—is stolen."

He looked at her in sheer amazement. It was clear enough that he did not, immediately, know what she was talking of. "The ring gone? Stolen, mother?"

Suddenly he burst into a laugh—so hearty, so spontaneous, so wholly foreign in its fine expression of good-natured raillery, to the tense atmosphere of accusation on the part of Mrs. Vanderlyn and supreme self-abnegation on the part of the old flute-player, which had, until this time, been vibrant in the room, that it seemed strangely, shockingly incongruous.

"John!" said his mother, in a tone of stern reproof, demanding of her son for the victim of misfortune consideration which she, herself, had scarcely shown, "you must not laugh. It is too heartless—right in this poor man's presence!"

This stopped his laughter, for it puzzled him. He looked from one of his companions to the other with an air of most complete bewilderment. "What's Herr Kreutzer got to do with it?" he asked.

"Why, he has just confessed."

"Confessed to what?"

"That he is guilty."

Kreutzer interrupted earnestly and hastily. He did not wish to have her even tell her son that Anna ever had been suspected. "Yes," he assured him earnestly, "I—I alone am guilty."

The youth's evident amazement doubled. Sinking into a chair he looked from his mother to Herr Kreutzer, from Herr Kreutzer to his mother, with an expression of bewilderment so genuine that, for the first time, his mother was a bit in doubt about her cleverness, for the first time Herr Kreutzer wondered if there might not, somewhere, be a ray of hope for him and for his Anna.

"Guilty of what?" said Vanderlyn, at length. "Of being the

father of the dearest girl in all the world, who has promised to become my wife?"

CHAPTER X

"Your wife!" cried Mrs. Vanderlyn. "Good heavens!" She sank back in her chair as much aghast as Kreutzer had been when she had amazed him by accusing Anna.

"And I bought that ring and gave it to her," John went on. "The dear girl! It's our engagement ring."

Kreutzer, who had been staring at him with the strained and anxious look of one who sees salvation just in sight, but cannot understand its aspect, quite, relaxed now and, also, sank into a chair.

"Oh, mine Gott sie dank!" he fervently exclaimed. "Mine Gott sie dank! You gave it to her! Oh, oh, oh, thank God!"

"Why certainly I gave it to her. It's our engagement ring. Bless her heart—she's promised me to wear it as soon as Herr Kreutzer gives consent."

Mrs. Vanderlyn found this too much for calm reception. She did not wish to, she would not believe.

"Why do you say such things?" she demanded of her son. "You're just trying to save him. Why did he confess?"

Kreutzer, now, looked at her with calm, cold dignity. His turn had come. Had she been a man he would have taken it with vehemence and pleasure; because she was not a man he took it with a careful self-repression but no lack of emphasis.

"I will tell you, Madame, why I made confession. It may be that you will not understand, but so it is. I told you that it had been I who stole the ring because I love my little girl so much that I would go to prison—ah, Madame, I would die!—rather than permit that she should suffer. For a mad moment, overborne by your amazing claims, I did believe that she had taken that ring. I thought that she had taken it to help her poor old father—the old flute-player who never has been able to give to his daughter what he wished to give, or what she deserved to have. I thought, perhaps, that Anna, swept away by sorrow for my struggling, had yielded to temptation to help *me*—the mistaken impulse of a loving child. No crime—no crime! I understand, now, what she meant when she was speaking with me. Her 'secret!' Her 'temptation!'"

He turned to John, now, and addressed him, solely. "Her 'temptation' was to be your wife when I had made her promise that she would not think of men until I came to her and told her that I had picked out the one for her. I see it, now; I see it. Her 'temptation'—it was only to become your wife!"

John laughed. "I'm mighty glad it was!" said he. "Yes; that was it; and it's all settled."

Mrs. Vanderlyn now rose in wrath. Was it credible that her own son, whom she had reared, as she had thought, to worship all the things she worshiped, wealth, position, rank, could have conceived an actual affection for this penniless, positionless, impossible flute-player's daughter?

"Settled that you marry her?" she cried. "The daughter of this old musician? It's impossible! Impossible!"

Her son looked at her deprecatingly. There was not a sign of yielding on his face, but there was plainly written there a keen desire to win her to his side. "Don't say that, mother," he implored, "I love—"

But she was not so easily to be placated. She had an argument to use, which, in her wrath, she fancied might be an effective one—and this showed that the poor lady did not even know her son.

"Your father left me all his money," she said viciously. "If you are fool enough to marry this girl, you shall have nothing—nothing!"

It did not seem to have, on the young man, the instantaneous effect which she had thought it would have. He merely looked at her with a grieved little frown, and, bending towards her, said with earnest emphasis: "*That* wouldn't make the slightest difference. I'm young and strong. We'll get along somehow—and we shall be together."

"You'll *starve* together!" she said viciously.

For a moment the two men remained in an embarrassed silence. Young Vanderlyn, with downcast eyes, was feeling greater mortification than he ever in his life had known before. Just then the loss of millions did not matter to him— what really distressed him was that his mother should make such an exhibition of cold-hearted snobbery before the father of the girl he loved.

"That wouldn't matter, mother, in the least," he said, at length. "Money! Do you think it possible that it would sway me? We won't starve together—quite. I'm strong—I am a man and I can do a man's work in the world. But you—remember, mother, you will have to take your choice between receiving Anna—and myself—together—or of being left alone."

Without another word he left the room—left it with an old man's dimmed and misty eyes agaze upon him, full of love and admiration.

Mrs. Vanderlyn rose, too, beside herself with shame and grief and indignation. She turned upon the flute-player.

"Alone!" she cried. "Did you hear that? Oh, the ingratitude, the selfishness, of children!"

"Madame," said Herr Kreutzer gravely, "do you not think he has a right to his own life—his happiness?"

"His happiness!" A rasping scorn was in the voice of the unhappy woman. "Nobody thinks of mine! He is my only son. He knows quite well that I can't live without him—that I could not give him up!"

Kreutzer smiled—not with an air of triumph—the discomfiture of the unhappy woman did not make him feel the least exultant. It was pure happiness that made him smile—joy to think that Anna's wedding would not, after all, be shadowed by her husband's sorrow for the loss of mother-love.

"Then Madame will yield?" he cried. "Madame will make the dear young people happy?"

"Upon one condition. Positively only upon one condition."

"What is that, Madame?"

"Your daughter, really, is charming."

"There I agree with you."

"She is wonderfully well-bred—I do not understand it. I could pass her, anywhere, for a distinguished foreigner—a foreigner of noble birth."

The father of the subject of her praise smiled gravely. "That is very true. She will—what you call it?—look the part."

"But to be quite frank," the lady went on "you, yourself, are quite impossible, Herr Kreutzer. Quite impossible, I must assure you."

"I, impossible? I—you say that I am quite impossible?"

She nodded very positively. "I don't like to hurt your feelings, my dear man; but I must make you understand. I can't have people saying that my dear son's father-in-law is a shabby old musician—a flute-player in a theatre. You see that clearly, don't you. How could I—"

"It is quite true," Herr Kreutzer admitted humbly. "I am a shabby old flute-player and you do not make it quite as bad as it is really, Madame." He looked at her and smiled a rueful smile. "It is not even a theatre in which I play, Madame, it is a beer-garden."

"A beer-garden!" she cried in horror. "Oh—Herr Kreutzer! Worse and worse!" Then, wheedlingly: "Listen. You say you love your daughter."

"Yes; surely; I love my daughter very dearly—almost as much, perhaps, as Madame loves her son. Almost. Almost."

"You would have gone to prison for her."

"Yes; to prison. Gladly would I go to prison for my Anna, if, by doing so, I could save her one moment's pain."

"Well, I'm going to suggest a thing not half so hard as that. I will give consent to my son's marriage to your daughter if you will agree to give her up entirely—to give her up *entirely*. You understand? You must never see her any more."

This was too much. The old man drew back with a cry of pain. "I give my Anna up! I never see her any more! Madame, do you know what you ask?"

She was not vividly impressed. "I suppose it may be hard, at first," she went on, casually, "but—"

He interrupted. "Hard! I am old—and poor. I have nothing—nothing—but that little girl. All my whole life long I work for her. My love for her has grown so close—close—close around my heart that from my breast you could not tear it out without, at the same time, tearing from that breast the heart itself. You hear, Madame? She is my soul—my life—all I have got—all—all—"

"But am I not giving up a great deal, too? I had hoped my son would marry well—perhaps, even, among the foreign nobility. That's what I took him off to Europe with me for. I'm simply wild to be presented at some court! Surely if I give all that up for my son's sake, you can do as much, at least, for Anna's."

"As much? Why, what you ask of me, Madame, is to abandon all!"

Mrs. Vanderlyn became impatient. It seemed to her that he was most unreasonable.

"I tell you that unless you do, I shall do nothing for them," she cried petulantly. "My son has no idea of money. He's never had to earn a dollar and he don't know how. They'll starve, if you don't yield, and it will be your fault—entirely your fault."

Herr Kreutzer bowed his head. His heart cried out within him at the horrible injustice of this woman, but, as he saw life, to yield was all that he could do. To stand in Anna's light, at this late day, when, all his life, he had, without the slightest thought of self, made sacrifices for her, would be too illogical, too utterly absurd. "Madame, I yield," he said. "I know too well what poverty can be—what misery! Yes, Madame, I will go. But sometimes I shall see her."

"Absolutely no!" said Mrs. Vanderlyn. "I'll run no risk of disagreeable comment. I have social enemies who would be too glad to pull me down. You must give her up to-day and go out of her life forever."

"I do not think she will consent to that. She, Madame—why, she loves her poor old father just a little."

"Of course, of course," she grudgingly admitted, "but she'll get over it. Ah, wait! I have it. You must find some way to make her think it's all your fault—that it's exactly what you want—"

"What I want! To give my little Anna up?"

"Certainly. If you are going to do it, you must burn your bridges behind you."

A big thought had been growing in Herr Kreutzer's mind. The execution of the plan which it suggested would involve the breaking of a resolution which had been unbroken for a score of years, but in emergency like this—

"Very well," said he. "Madame, my bridges burn!"

"You'll do it?"

"You shall see."

With a firm step and an erectness of fine carriage which surprised the weak, self-centred woman who was watching him, he stepped, now, to the door, and, opening it, called loudly:

"Come, sir."

For a moment, after he had reached it, he stopped to listen, for from the lower hallway came the sounds of altercation. He waited till a curse or two had died away, until the thudding of a heavy body on the boards was heard. It merely meant a fight, and fights were not uncommon in the tenement. He stepped out into the hall. "Come, sir," he called into the darkness.

A bounding step upon the stair responded and an instant later John entered, anxious faced and fixing his entreating eyes immovably upon his mother. He was a bit dishevelled.

"Excuse me," he said nervously. "I had to settle with Moresco. He was the officer you had. I'll have to pay a little fine, I guess; but it was worth it. What have you—decided, mother?"

"Your mother," Kreutzer said, before she had a chance to

speak, "has given her consent."

John went to her with beaming face and caught her hands. "You're a brick, mother." Gaily he caught her in his arms.

His transport was rudely interrupted, though, by Kreutzer's voice, this time so harsh, so stern, so utterly unlike the old flute-player's usual genial tone that he was startled.

"But I, sir," he said raspingly, "I—I have, myself, something to say."

Son and mother looked at the new Kreutzer (for, suddenly, an utter change had come upon the man: he was majestic) with amazement, almost with alarm. He paid no heed to them but went firmly to the kitchen door.

"Anna, Anna," he called sternly. "Come, I want you. I have something which I wish to say."

Hurriedly the girl came in, looking at him wonderingly. Never in her life had she heard such a tone from her father's lips before.

"Anna, you love this man—Herr Vanderlyn?"

"Yes, father; I—I love him. Yes."

"You love him very, very much?" His voice, now, softened somewhat.

"More than I could ever tell you, father."

She turned her eyes from the old flute-player's to those of the young man, and smiled at him.

"Anna!" he exclaimed, and started towards her from his mother's side.

"Stop!" said Kreutzer and held up his hand. Then, turning again to Anna: "You would not even give him up for me?"

"You would not ask that of me, father," she said confidently, "for it is my happiness."

The old German nodded slowly, somewhat sadly. "No," he admitted, "no; I would not ask it.... You shall have—your happiness." He straightened, then, and looked as her so differently that it startled her a little. "But I, Anna," he said sorrowfully, "I go from your life—forever."

She stood, amazed. What could this mean? At first she thought he might be making game of her, but the look of bitter sorrow on his face convinced her that this could not be. "You, father!" she exclaimed. "No; I will not allow it! Why—why—"

She made a move as if to cast her arms around his neck in her appeal. He stepped back to avoid her and held his hand up warningly.

"Do not touch me," he said, chokingly. "I must be strong—strong enough, my little one, to tell you. Ah, my little girl, I go out of your life; but I shall not forget! I shall remember all our songs, and the old flute—when I play the old flute, Anna, always shall I think of you."

She would not be held back, but ran to him and put her hand upon his arm and thus stood, looking up into his face with pleading eyes.

"I will not give you up!" she cried. "You shall not go!

Why ... why ..."

Here was the opportunity for which the old man had been waiting; here was his chance to pay in full for every pang, the haughty woman who had so egregiously insulted his and him; here the chance to show a parvenu her place—and yet to do these things without discourtesy. Drawing himself up proudly, without the scornful look which one of less fine sensibility might have thrown at her in similar circumstances, he gave his calm and dignified explanation with the air of a true prince.

"It is because," said he, "that in my family no father ever has allowed his daughter to marry any one who is not by birth her equal."

There could be no mistaking the amazement which his words aroused among his hearers. Anna and the youth who held her hand looked at him in frank surprise; but it was on the face of Mrs. Vanderlyn that most emotion showed. It was plain that the grand lady found it hard to credit what her ears assured her they had heard. Upon the ship she had remarked that Kreutzer looked as if he might belong to a distinguished family. Now his attitude and carriage were the attitude and carriage of a king—a dignified, but kind and gentle king; not arrogant, as her instincts would have made her in like circumstances, but stately and—decisive. The aristocracy of centuries expressed itself in his straight back; his face was that of one born over-lord of thousands; his steady and unwavering glance was that of a real Personage looking kindly but not with any fellowship upon a commoner, as it calmly swung from its intent pause on his daughter's face to hers.

"Of equal birth!" said she, amazed. "Why, what—"

"Madame," said he, with no abatement of his kindly dignity, "I must explain some things. My life has been a very hard one and my Anna has been all which made it livable. When her mother died—there were objections to the marriage and I also had some wicked enemies—they would have taken my dear child from me. Twenty years of dread of this, of dodging and evasion like a fugitive, in humble places have succeeded. Had they found me, then I might have lost my Anna, for her mother's relatives, who hate me, they are very, very powerful. I have worried, worried, worried, ever, lest I lose her. Even have I had to hide my little artistry in my profession because, had I exploited it, it would have told my enemies where they could find me. Such has been the life which I have led because I loved my daughter.

"Madame," he went on, not patronizingly but with a growing consciousness of his own impregnable position which impressed even the self-seeking woman he addressed, "to you I am only Kreutzer, the poor flute-player; but in my native country I am more—Count Otto Von Lichtenstahl."

"Good heavens!" she cried. "The man is mad!"

"No, Madame. I have been unfortunate. I have not even told my Anna of my title, because I have not wished to make her feel unhappy. It is so long since I have lived as would befit my rank, that, almost, I had quite forgotten it; but always I have kept the proofs."

From an inner pocket of his coat the old man drew a worn cloth envelope which held long, folded papers.

"Look, Madame."

Almost as one who dreams she took the little packet from his hand and hastily glanced through the papers which comprised it. Though evidently somewhat impressed her doubts still remained.

"It is easy to manufacture such documents," she said finally. "How am I to know that these are genuine?"

The old man, wounded to the quick, made no reply, but looked at her with a silent dignity and stern reproof that affected her more than any words could have. It was evident that his pent-up indignation, however, was on the point of breaking forth; but what he might have said must always remain mystery, for at that moment, M'riar entered, a large, impressive envelope held in her hand.

"Postman's bean 'ere," she explained, and held it toward the old musician.

As Herr Kreutzer saw this letter he gasped with astonishment and, taking it eagerly from her hand, quickly tore it open. As he read it great joy showed upon his face. He stood transfigured, speechless. At last he handed it to Mrs. Vanderlyn.

"Perhaps Madame will believe this," he said quietly.

Mrs. Vanderlyn gave an ecstatic little cry after her first glance at the imposing document.

"The Imperial Seal!" she exclaimed. "A letter from the Emperor himself!

"But, what is this?" she continued, as she read farther. "He speaks about a pardon. What have you done, Herr Kreutzer?"

"It is very simple, Madame," he replied. "Now that I have this, now I can tell all. It had been necessary, as I have explained, that my marriage to my dear Anna's mother be kept secret. When, after one short year, she died, as I have already told you, all came to light.

"I was an officer in His Majesty's Imperial guards. One day a fellow officer, an enemy who had always hated me, insulted me because of my marriage—insulted the memory of my dead wife. There was a duel. He fell, as I thought, mortally wounded. The law was strict against participants in duels, and because I could not be parted from my little Anna I took her in my arms and we left Prussia—I believed forever. But at last the Emperor has relented and has pardoned me. He calls me back to Prussia! Ah, it is like him! He has not forgotten!"

"Were you such friends?" asked Mrs. Vanderlyn with awe.

"We were schoolmates at the College in Bonn," he answered. "We have drunk the hoffbrau together—in a beer garden."

Gone was all the scorn of Mrs. Vanderlyn. Quite forgotten, to all outward seeming, were her apprehensions lest the old musician's daughter might be unworthy of her son, her fears lest the old man, himself, should prove to be a handicap upon her social aspirations. She was still running through the papers, and, it must be said, with real intelligence and under-standing, and her face was beaming with delight. It was as if from the beginning she had favored him and Anna and was now delighted to find confirmation of the confidence which she had felt in them.

"How absolutely splendid!" she exclaimed. "John, it is really true. I know my Almanach de Gotha—all the titles." Turning, now, to Kreutzer, she beamed upon him with a cordial smile which plainly took no count of all the frowns which, in the past few minutes, she had sent in his direction. "But Lichtenstahl is a magnificent estate. How does it happen that you—"

"The estate was lost to me, Madame, through the folly of my ancestors; but—their pride I have inherited. Therefore, although I know that I cannot prevent this marriage, I will not give consent to it." He turned, now, to his daughter. "Rather, Anna, I go from your life forever!"

"You shall not!" the girl cried. "You are my dear, kind father. I won't let you go alone. I'll stay with you, close beside you, while you live."

She threw herself into his arms and Kreutzer, there enfolding her, looked proudly out above the wonderful bowed head of the distressed and sobbing girl at Mrs. Vanderlyn. This time there was a note of triumph in his voice—a note of triumph which had not been there, even when he had made the announcement of the glory of his birth and family.

Mrs. Vanderlyn looked at them in chagrin. A slow flush spread upon her face.

"*Now*, mother," her son asked, "what have you to say?"

She forced a sigh as of a self-effacing resignation, but upon her face there lurked, in spite of her, a little smirk of satisfaction—of snobbery which had been gratified, at last, after many disappointments. Her manner had changed utterly. Her tones were honeyed, now; her glance was quite as sweetly motherly as she could make it as she looked from Anna to her questioner and back again.

"What have I to say? My boy, I cannot let you lose your happiness.... And the dear man's confession has made everything so different!" An ecstatic smile spread on her face. "Why, John, he is a friend of the dear Emperor!" She turned, now, again to Kreutzer. Everything considered she made good weather of it on a difficult occasion. "My dear Count," she pleaded, "won't you reconsider, please?"

The old flute-player shook his head. "I do not wish to hurt your feelings, Madame, but it is impossible—impossible."

"Mother," said John Vanderlyn, not viciously, but, still, a little wickedly, "you are up against it. He'll never reconsider."

"But he must! He must!" said Mrs. Vanderlyn, entirely capitulating. "There is nothing I won't do!" She turned, imploringly, to Kreutzer. "Listen. To-night I hold a reception. It shall be in your daughter's honor and I will, while it is going on, announce her engagement to my son." She took the ring which the flute-player had passed over to her, and, holding it between her thumb and forefinger, advanced towards Anna with it. "See, I will, myself, put on the ring."

John protested, though, at this. "No, mother," he said hastily, "I will attend to that."

He took the ring from her reluctant fingers, and, raising Anna's hand, slipped it into place in open token of betrothal. Then, with an air of manly resolution the young man turned to the father. "And I'll do more," he said. "You and Anna shall not be parted. I'll buy the old estate of Lichtenstahl and you shall be its master, as you ought to be, as long as your life lasts. You'll let us be your guests, perhaps, and there we'll all be happy. Eh?"

"I beg you to consider the happiness of our children," Mrs. Vanderlyn said humbly.

Herr Kreutzer smiled. Conditions, now, were different

indeed. No longer was he scorned as a poor flute-player, unworthy to become connected with the house of Vanderlyn by marriage.

"Ah," said he, "you beg of me! Well, that is different. Your happiness, my little Anna ... so ... I will see. Only give me just a little time to think of it alone."

"Of course," said Mrs. Vanderlyn, with a deep sigh of relief. "Come, Anna darling, we must get home in time to dress for the reception. My dear Count, I'll send the motor back for you. You'll surely come?"

"Perhaps I come," said he indifferently. "Possibly."

But he turned to Anna with a beaming face on which love shone, triumphant. "At least, my Anna, it is not goodbye— and that is very good. *Nichtwahr*?"

"No, father; it could never be goodbye with us. Together always, father—always—always—us—together."

She ran to him and hid her head upon his breast.

A moment later and the girl had been borne off by Mrs. Vanderlyn in triumph. John gave his hand to Kreutzer and the aged flute-player pressed it, smiling at him with approval.

As his future son-in-law went out the old man stood and gazed long at the open door. Upon his face there were the lines of happiness, not worry, as there had been for so many years, not bitter grief as there had been that day.

There came a clatter on the stairs which broke the reverie which held him, and he stepped forward to the door, peering out into the hall to see the cause of the unusual noise. An officer approached, and, tightly gripped by her right arm, he held M'riar.

"Say," said he gruffly. "You Mr. Krootzer? Wot? Yes? Well, this kid comes to the station-house and hollers that she's stole a ring and somebody that ain't had anything to do with it is gettin' pinched fer stealin' it. The kid acts plumb bug-house, but Sarge he says fer me to come around and see wot's up. Wot is she, dippy? Did she re'ly steal a di'mond? This don't look like wot you'd call a likely place to find a di'mond."

"No," said Herr Kreutzer, after he had had sufficient time to sense the meaning of the officer's strange statement, "she did not steal a diamond, or anything. It was good of you to bring her home to me. The dear child—she suffers from,—er— what you call emotional insanity, I think. A little too much love for an old man and his daughter, possibly. That is what I think. It is nothing worse than that. Thank you, very much, for bringing her to me. Take this, sir, for your trouble." He handed him, with bland benevolence, his last dollar.

"Say, I'm gettin' it a good deal better than the cop wot come here to this house a while ago. He's bein' stuck together at the hospital in a dozen places, they tell me. He's like a jigsaw puzzle."

"Ah, I wonder what could have occurred to him."

The officer went down the stairs.

"Come in, my child," the flute-player invited M'riar. "Soon you will be better, doubtless. Yes, I feel quite certain that you will be better, soon."

He softly closed the door behind them.

"M'riar," he said slowly, "sit down by me. I think I play you something—just a little something—on my flute."

"My heye!" said M'riar, entranced.

"But no," said Kreutzer. "First come to me. Ah, give me a kiss. Always shall you have a home with me or with my Anna."

Spellbound, after he had kissed her, she sat close by his feet upon the floor until he finished playing and laid down the flute. "I s'y!" she murmured, then.

THE END

Edward Marshall and Charles T. Dazey

Choose from Thousands of 1stWorldLibrary Classics By

A. M. Barnard
Ada Leverson
Adolphus William Ward
Aesop
Agatha Christie
Alexander Aaronsohn
Alexander Kielland
Alexandre Dumas
Alfred Gatty
Alfred Ollivant
Alice Duer Miller
Alice Turner Curtis
Alice Dunbar
Allen Chapman
Alleyne Ireland
Ambrose Bierce
Amelia E. Barr
Amory H. Bradford
Andrew Lang
Andrew McFarland Davis
Andy Adams
Angela Brazil
Anna Alice Chapin
Anna Sewell
Annie Besant
Annie Hamilton Donnell
Annie Payson Call
Annie Roe Carr
Annonaymous
Anton Chekhov
Archibald Lee Fletcher
Arnold Bennett
Arthur C. Benson
Arthur Conan Doyle
Arthur M. Winfield
Arthur Ransome
Arthur Schnitzler
Arthur Train
Atticus
B.H. Baden-Powell
B. M. Bower
B. C. Chatterjee
Baroness Emmuska Orczy
Baroness Orczy
Basil King
Bayard Taylor
Ben Macomber
Bertha Muzzy Bower
Bjornstjerne Bjornson

Booth Tarkington
Boyd Cable
Bram Stoker
C. Collodi
C. E. Orr
C. M. Ingleby
Carolyn Wells
Catherine Parr Traill
Charles A. Eastman
Charles Amory Beach
Charles Dickens
Charles Dudley Warner
Charles Farrar Browne
Charles Ives
Charles Kingsley
Charles Klein
Charles Hanson Towne
Charles Lathrop Pack
Charles Romyn Dake
Charles Whibley
Charles Willing Beale
Charlotte M. Braeme
Charlotte M. Yonge
Charlotte Perkins Stetson
Clair W. Hayes
Clarence Day Jr.
Clarence E. Mulford
Clemence Housman
Confucius
Coningsby Dawson
Cornelis DeWitt Wilcox
Cyril Burleigh
D. H. Lawrence
Daniel Defoe
David Garnett
Dinah Craik
Don Carlos Janes
Donald Keyhoe
Dorothy Kilner
Dougan Clark
Douglas Fairbanks
E. Nesbit
E. P. Roe
E. Phillips Oppenheim
E. S. Brooks
Earl Barnes
Edgar Rice Burroughs
Edith Van Dyne
Edith Wharton

Edward Everett Hale
Edward J. O'Biren
Edward S. Ellis
Edwin L. Arnold
Eleanor Atkins
Eleanor Hallowell Abbott
Eliot Gregory
Elizabeth Gaskell
Elizabeth McCracken
Elizabeth Von Arnim
Ellem Key
Emerson Hough
Emilie F. Carlen
Emily Bronte
Emily Dickinson
Enid Bagnold
Enilor Macartney Lane
Erasmus W. Jones
Ernie Howard Pie
Ethel May Dell
Ethel Turner
Ethel Watts Mumford
Eugene Sue
Eugenie Foa
Eugene Wood
Eustace Hale Ball
Evelyn Everett-green
Everard Cotes
F. H. Cheley
F. J. Cross
F. Marion Crawford
Fannie E. Newberry
Federick Austin Ogg
Ferdinand Ossendowski
Fergus Hume
Florence A. Kilpatrick
Fremont B. Deering
Francis Bacon
Francis Darwin
Frances Hodgson Burnett
Frances Parkinson Keyes
Frank Gee Patchin
Frank Harris
Frank Jewett Mather
Frank L. Packard
Frank V. Webster
Frederic Stewart Isham
Frederick Trevor Hill
Frederick Winslow Taylor

Friedrich Kerst
Friedrich Nietzsche
Fyodor Dostoyevsky
G.A. Henty
G.K. Chesterton
Gabrielle E. Jackson
Garrett P. Serviss
Gaston Leroux
George A. Warren
George Ade
Geroge Bernard Shaw
George Cary Eggleston
George Durston
George Ebers
George Eliot
George Gissing
George MacDonald
George Meredith
George Orwell
George Sylvester Viereck
George Tucker
George W. Cable
George Wharton James
Gertrude Atherton
Gordon Casserly
Grace E. King
Grace Gallatin
Grace Greenwood
Grant Allen
Guillermo A. Sherwell
Gulielma Zollinger
Gustav Flaubert
H. A. Cody
H. B. Irving
H. C. Bailey
H. G. Wells
H. H. Munro
H. Irving Hancock
H. R. Naylor
H. Rider Haggard
H. W. C. Davis
Haldeman Julius
Hall Caine
Hamilton Wright Mabie
Hans Christian Andersen
Harold Avery
Harold McGrath
Harriet Beecher Stowe
Harry Castlemon
Harry Coghill
Harry Houidini

Hayden Carruth
Helent Hunt Jackson
Helen Nicolay
Hendrik Conscience
Hendy David Thoreau
Henri Barbusse
Henrik Ibsen
Henry Adams
Henry Ford
Henry Frost
Henry James
Henry Jones Ford
Henry Seton Merriman
Henry W Longfellow
Herbert A. Giles
Herbert Carter
Herbert N. Casson
Herman Hesse
Hildegard G. Frey
Homer
Honore De Balzac
Horace B. Day
Horace Walpole
Horatio Alger Jr.
Howard Pyle
Howard R. Garis
Hugh Lofting
Hugh Walpole
Humphry Ward
Ian Maclaren
Inez Haynes Gillmore
Irving Bacheller
Isabel Cecilia Williams
Isabel Hornibrook
Israel Abrahams
Ivan Turgenev
J. G.Austin
J. Henri Fabre
J. M. Barrie
J. M. Walsh
J. Macdonald Oxley
J. R. Miller
J. S. Fletcher
J. S. Knowles
J. Storer Clouston
J. W. Duffield
Jack London
Jacob Abbott
James Allen
James Andrews
James Baldwin

James Branch Cabell
James DeMille
James Joyce
James Lane Allen
James Lane Allen
James Oliver Curwood
James Oppenheim
James Otis
James R. Driscoll
Jane Abbott
Jane Austen
Jane L. Stewart
Janet Aldridge
Jens Peter Jacobsen
Jerome K. Jerome
Jessie Graham Flower
John Buchan
John Burroughs
John Cournos
John F. Kennedy
John Gay
John Glasworthy
John Habberton
John Joy Bell
John Kendrick Bangs
John Milton
John Philip Sousa
John Taintor Foote
Jonas Lauritz Idemil Lie
Jonathan Swift
Joseph A. Altsheler
Joseph Carey
Joseph Conrad
Joseph E. Badger Jr
Joseph Hergesheimer
Joseph Jacobs
Jules Vernes
Julian Hawthrone
Julie A Lippmann
Justin Huntly McCarthy
Kakuzo Okakura
Karle Wilson Baker
Kate Chopin
Kenneth Grahame
Kenneth McGaffey
Kate Langley Bosher
Kate Langley Bosher
Katherine Cecil Thurston
Katherine Stokes
L. A. Abbot
L. T. Meade

L. Frank Baum
Latta Griswold
Laura Dent Crane
Laura Lee Hope
Laurence Housman
Lawrence Beasley
Leo Tolstoy
Leonid Andreyev
Lewis Carroll
Lewis Sperry Chafer
Lilian Bell
Lloyd Osbourne
Louis Hughes
Louis Joseph Vance
Louis Tracy
Louisa May Alcott
Lucy Fitch Perkins
Lucy Maud Montgomery
Luther Benson
Lydia Miller Middleton
Lyndon Orr
M. Corvus
M. H. Adams
Margaret E. Sangster
Margret Howth
Margaret Vandercook
Margaret W. Hungerford
Margret Penrose
Maria Edgeworth
Maria Thompson Daviess
Mariano Azuela
Marion Polk Angellotti
Mark Overton
Mark Twain
Mary Austin
Mary Catherine Crowley
Mary Cole
Mary Hastings Bradley
Mary Roberts Rinehart
Mary Rowlandson
M. Wollstonecraft Shelley
Maud Lindsay
Max Beerbohm
Myra Kelly
Nathaniel Hawthrone
Nicolo Machiavelli
O. F. Walton
Oscar Wilde

Owen Johnson
P.G. Wodehouse
Paul and Mabel Thorne
Paul G. Tomlinson
Paul Severing
Percy Brebner
Percy Keese Fitzhugh
Peter B. Kyne
Plato
Quincy Allen
R. Derby Holmes
R. L. Stevenson
R. S. Ball
Rabindranath Tagore
Rahul Alvares
Ralph Bonehill
Ralph Henry Barbour
Ralph Victor
Ralph Waldo Emmerson
Rene Descartes
Ray Cummings
Rex Beach
Rex E. Beach
Richard Harding Davis
Richard Jefferies
Richard Le Gallienne
Robert Barr
Robert Frost
Robert Gordon Anderson
Robert L. Drake
Robert Lansing
Robert Lynd
Robert Michael Ballantyne
Robert W. Chambers
Rosa Nouchette Carey
Rudyard Kipling
Saint Augustine
Samuel B. Allison
Samuel Hopkins Adams
Sarah Bernhardt
Sarah C. Hallowell
Selma Lagerlof
Sherwood Anderson
Sigmund Freud
Standish O'Grady
Stanley Weyman
Stella Benson
Stella M. Francis

Stephen Crane
Stewart Edward White
Stijn Streuvels
Swami Abhedananda
Swami Parmananda
T. S. Ackland
T. S. Arthur
The Princess Der Ling
Thomas A. Janvier
Thomas A Kempis
Thomas Anderton
Thomas Bailey Aldrich
Thomas Bulfinch
Thomas De Quincey
Thomas Dixon
Thomas H. Huxley
Thomas Hardy
Thomas More
Thornton W. Burgess
U. S. Grant
Upton Sinclair
Valentine Williams
Various Authors
Vaughan Kester
Victor Appleton
Victor G. Durham
Victoria Cross
Virginia Woolf
Wadsworth Camp
Walter Camp
Walter Scott
Washington Irving
Wilbur Lawton
Wilkie Collins
Willa Cather
Willard F. Baker
William Dean Howells
William le Queux
W. Makepeace Thackeray
William W. Walter
William Shakespeare
Winston Churchill
Yei Theodora Ozaki
Yogi Ramacharaka
Young E. Allison
Zane Grey

www.ingramcontent.com/pod-product-compliance
Lightning Source LLC
Chambersburg PA
CBHW022156260626
47155CB00018B/2084